DAKSHIN

VEGETARIAN
CUISINE
FROM
SOUTH

Dakshin

Vegetarian
Cuisine
from
South

INDIA

CHANDRA PADMANABHAN

PERIPLUS

Dedication

To my family and friends, who are too numerous to be named.
To those who taught me the rudiments of cooking —
though they are no longer with me today, their traditions live on.

~

First published in India in 1992 as *Dakshin:*
Vegetarian Delicacies from South India
Copyright © Chandra Padmanabhan 1992
First published in Australia by Angus&Robertson Publishers in 1994

Recipes copyright © Chandra Padmanabhan 1994
Adaptation and photographs copyright © HarperCollins*Publishers* Pty Limited 1994

Periplus Editions
with Editorial offices at 153 Milk Street Boston, MA 02109
Published in 1999 by arrangement with HarperCollins*Publishers* Australia.
Reprinted in 2002, 2004

ISBN 962-593-527-4

Distributed by:

NORTH AMERICA, LATIN AMERICA
& EUROPE
Tuttle Publishing
Distribution Center
Airport Industrial Park
364 Innovation Drive
North Claredon, VT 05759-9436
Tel: (802) 773-8930
Tel: (800) 773 6993

ASIA PACIFIC
Berkeley Books Pte. Ltd.
130 Joo Seng Road
#06-01/03 Olivine Building
Singapore 368357
Tel: (65) 6280-1330
Fax:(65) 6280-6290

JAPAN
Tuttle Publishing
Yaehari Bldg., 3F
5-4-12 Osaki, Shinagawa-ku
Tokyo 141 0032
Tel: (03) 5437-0171
Fax: (03) 5437-0755

Photography by Jon Bader, Stylist Georgina Dolling
Produced by Phoenix Offset and printed in China

ACKNOWLEDGMENTS

~

The author would like to acknowledge the following people for their assistance:

Beena Mathews
Mythili Varadarajan
Nalini Ramakrishna
Neela Srinivasamurthy
Padma Nagarajan
P. Raghupathi
Sarayu Ramaswamy
Shanti Krishnamurty
Sharada Rajamani
S. Shobana
Sreela Kowsik
Subashree Krishnaswamy
Uma Narayanan
Vijayalakshmi Kamat
P. Vasumathi

The publishers would also like to thank the following contributors for their generosity in supplying props for photography:

Joan Bowers Antiques,
56–64 Palmer Street,
Woolloomooloo, Sydney

Carol Selva Rajah of
Gourmet Asian Cuisine,
Wollstonecraft, Sydney

Community Aid Abroad,
Manly, Sydney

Miriam Elshaikh

Special thanks to Robin Rajan and
Rajesh Kalra of the Raaj Indian Brasserie, Sydney

CONTENTS

PREFACE

When I started cooking over twenty-five years ago, I never really thought that I would enjoy it so much. Over the years, my recipes, written down hastily on odd scraps of paper, have found their way into the kitchens of my relatives and friends, most of whom were young girls on the threshold of marriage. For some time now, they have been insisting that I get my recipes together. The result is this book, a simple introduction to basic South Indian vegetarian cooking.

Our cooking never makes use of exact weights and measures. We are taught to cultivate a sense of smell and colour, and to achieve perfection through experimenting. Almost every ingredient is measured only by hand. I have standardised the weights and measures here, though, to make this book easy to use. As in most other families, my recipes are my family's own, handed down over generations. A few, of course, are special gifts given to me by friends. Though traditional and authentic, these recipes have been simplified and shortened to suit our modern needs, keeping in mind that electric blenders and food processors have replaced the mortar and pestle in the modern kitchen.

A word on the tempering, which gives the dishes a crunchy, nutty flavour. It is typical of all South Indian cooking. At first glance, it may seem as if it is nothing more than a few mustard seeds spluttering and a couple of dals turning golden in colour. However, it is this delicate blending of spices that imparts the distinctive aroma of each dish. The spices are roasted, ground or popped whole into hot oil. Mastery over seasonings can make all the difference.

From the points of view of both nutrition and health, South Indian cooking is perfectly balanced — low both in fat and cholesterol. Most of the vegetables are steamed or cooked on a low heat. Oil is used sparingly and a variety of protein-rich dals form a part of the daily menu. A meal is always finished off with wholesome and soothing homemade yogurt.

I have tried as far as possible to give English equivalents for South Indian names. Since I am most familiar with Tamil, the South Indian names I have used are predominantly from the language. However, most recipes are common to all South Indians, with minor variations, of course.

Most of the receipes serve exactly four members of my own family. However, this quantity may serve six people in your family. The quantities spices used in the recipes suit my family and friends. Feel free to add more or to decrease the amounts, particularly that of the chillies (chili peppers). A word of advice: if you decrease the quantity of chillies, make sure you decrease accordingly the quantity of salt and souring agent.

Even the methods given for recipes need not be scrupulously followed. The joy of cooking lies in experimenting. I do, however, recommend you go through the short introductory notes before trying out any recipe.

I invite you to share with me my favourite recipes.

CHANDRA PADMANABHAN

IMPORTANT NOTES

~

Experienced cooks measure almost all ingredients by hand. They know instinctively the right amount required. To make it easy for the beginner, I have measured most ingredients by volume rather than by weight. I have used the standard cups, tablespoons and teaspoons found in most kitchens today.

A word of caution: while trying out a recipe, make sure you use the same measure for all the ingredients. For example, if a recipe requires three different types of flour, make sure you use the same cup to measure all three.

Throughout this book, the following weight and measure equivalents have been used as standard:

Measures

	METRIC	US/IMPERIAL
1 cup	250 ml	8 fl oz
½ cup	125 ml	4 fl oz
¼ cup	60 ml	2 fl oz

Weights

	METRIC	IMPERIAL
	125 g	4 oz (¼ lb)
	250 g (¼ kg)	8 oz (½ lb)
	500 g (½ kg)	16 oz (1 lb)
	1000 g (1 kg)	32 oz (2 lbs)
	1500 g (1½ kg)	48 oz (3 lbs)

Listed below are equivalents for cup and tablespoon measures. Please note that any small differences between metric, US and imperial measures have been absorbed, and will not affect the recipes

Equivalent Cup and Spoon Measures

(all countries use the same teaspoon measures)

	UNITED STATES	UNITED KINGDOM	AUSTRALIA	NEW ZEALAND
1 tablespoon	15 ml (½ fl oz)	15 ml (½ fl oz)	20 ml	15 ml
1 cup 240 ml (7 fl oz)	250 ml (8 fl oz)	250 ml	250 ml	250 ml

Cooking with Dals

In India, lentils and pulses (i.e. dried peas and beans) are commonly known as 'dal'. Before cooking with dal, you will need to pick out any foreign matter, and rinse well, using a sieve and fresh, cold water.

In South Indian cuisine, dals are not normally soaked before cooking, unless they are to be ground into a paste. If not stipulated in the recipe, do not soak dals before using. South Indian cooking is known for its 'tempering' and for the crunchy, nutty flavour of the dals used. If these are soaked before cooking, this texture and taste is lost.

INTRODUCTION

India, it is often said, is an experience. Complex and fascinating, it is ablaze with traditions, people, crafts, colours, wildlife and food. A veritable kaleidoscope with every little detail of life so startlingly different, so uniquely its own.

Take South India, tucked away snugly below the Vindhya and Satpura mountain ranges, which roughly divide India into two. This chunk of land that extends across the Deccan Peninsula, a remnant of a once large and stable plateau, is nothing like its northern counterpart. Fringed by coastal plains, traversed by rocky plateaus, fertile river valleys, lush tropical forests and hardy mountainous terrain, it has an entirely different story to tell. Its four states and one union territory — Tamil Nadu, Karnataka, Andhra Pradesh, Kerala and Pondicherry — have their own language and culture, customs and heritage, architecture and handicrafts. In fact, it isn't even very wise to club these states together since ethnic variations are so apparent that even within each state, every little community has its own way of doing things, totally at variance with another.

Yet, one perceives a common heritage, a discernible unity, especially in the vegetarian cuisine of the four states. Of course, there are innumerable area specialities. For example, the little town of Udipi is the home of the golden brown, crisp Masala Dosai, which is justly renowned the world over. Today, of course, every single self-respecting South Indian will swear by her or his own family recipe for the scrumptious dosais. Almost every household will tell you about a secret ingredient — a great-grandmother's legacy — for almost any dish. Despite native diversities, the pattern of eating is much the same in the whole of the south.

First of all we eat with our hands, the right hand to be precise, serving ourselves at the table and picking up our glasses of water with our left hand. It's almost sacrilege to use cutlery and, believe me, South Indian food never tastes as good as when you lick it off your fingers.

Rice, of course, is the queen of grains and makes its almost ubiquitous appearance, in one or more forms, in almost every meal. Lentils or dals are also very important since they form a bulk of protein in a vegetarian diet. These two staples, together or alone, are used in a variety of mouth-watering ways — pounded, ground, fermented, boiled and sautéed.

A typical meal consists of three courses — rice with sambar, rasam and yogurt (Indian curd). The rice is generally served steaming hot and pearly white.

Sambars, tart and thick, can be made with tamarind, dal, and buttermilk. Some kind of vegetable is usually boiled along with the base. It is mixed with just enough rice to absorb the juices and dollops of ghee, so that neat little balls of rice can be popped into the mouth.

The next course, the *rasam*, is watery and soupy. It is customary to wet the rice completely with the rasam before it is eaten. With their judicious combination of tamarind and tomatoes, rasams have a piquant, tangy taste which lends itself to drinking it straight.

The last course is always the soothing, gentle curd rice, so good for the stomach. Made with homemade yogurt, it is the perfect way to end a satisfying meal.

Vegetable dishes called *poriyals*, generally stir-fried gently or sautéed to a golden crispness, are served as accompaniments. As are the versatile *kootus* — not too dry, not too wet. Salads, pickles and poppadoms — either fried or roasted — are always served on the side.

A meal is always carefully planned, blending and balancing colours, textures, flavours and nutritional contents. If, for example, the sambar is hot and rich, a more bland vegetable dish is served by way of contrast.

Our snacks, called *tiffins*, occupy a special place in South Indian cooking. More often than not, they are a complete meal in themselves. Crunchy, spicy, sweet or fiery hot, they can be served at almost any time of the day.

Most of our desserts and sweet treats are so delicious, yet so simple to make. For festive occasions, *payasams* are a must. More often than not, jaggery (an unrefined sugar) is used as the sweetening agent. Less sweet than sugar, jaggery has an indescribable earthy flavour. There is a whole variety of treats for the sweet tooth — liquids, pancakes, crisp munchies and soft, melting, yummy sweets or candies. Some can be stored for days in airtight containers.

Pickles and chutneys are a South Indian speciality. They can be made with almost anything. With mango alone, you can make as many as twelve different kinds of pickles. Ask anyone from Andhra Pradesh — the home of pickes and chutneys.

Coconut, you will notice, is an important and almost integral ingredient. South India's entire coastline is dotted with swaying coconut palms. Both coconut and copra (the dried flesh of coconuts) are used in a million imaginative ways, either sparingly or abundantly.

Good cooking is all in the seasoning, caution our grandmothers. They couldn't be more right. Though South Indian cooking is subtly flavoured and mildly spiced, it nevertheless contains a delectable blend of spices used in ingenious ways. It's therefore not really surprising to find a shelf full of seasonings in any home in South India, since it is the land of spices. It is these spices, in fact, which changed the history of India.

Even in earlier times, intrepid traders landed along the coast of South India, lured by the haunting aroma of spices. Later, when Vasco De Gama unfurled his sails, circled the Cape of Good Hope and landed in Calicut, the benign local ruler innocently offered trade. That one act set off a virtual stampede from Europe, with the Dutch, Portuguese, French, and the English elbowing out one another in order to capture the lucrative spice trade. Almost any spice you care to name can be and is grown in South India — cardamom, pepper, nutmeg, mace, ginger, asafoetida. The list just goes on and on.

Many people associate India with tea drinking, so it may surprise some people to find that South Indians also take their coffee drinking very seriously. The coffee beans, grown mainly in the lush hills of the state of Karnataka, are roasted and ground to make strong, aromatic filtered coffee.

Even from this small introduction, it is easy to see that South Indian cuisine is subtly flavoured, yet rich in variety. Enjoy the excellent fare.

SAMBARS

Thick and fiery, sambars are the first course in any South Indian meal. Serve them steaming hot with plain cooked rice, vegetable accompaniments and poppadoms, either fried or roasted. A dollop of bubbling ghee adds a flavour of its own.

~

Sambars can have any one of three bases: tamarind; tamarind and dal; or buttermilk. Almost any vegetable can be used in a sambar. The tart tamarind juice, besides having a cooling effect, has the unique property of preserving the vitamins of the vegetables cooked in it.

~

Sambar powders are an essential item seen on the spice shelf of any home in South India. If you do not wish to make your own sambar powder, you can buy good-quality ready-made powders in spice shops, Indian markets or Asian food stores.

ORDINARY SAMBAR
Kuzhambu

PREPARATION TIME: 20 MIN. COOKING TIME: 2 HRS
SERVES 4

*½ cup (3 oz) red gram dal (pigeon peas, toor dal),
picked over and rinsed
2 cups (16 fl oz) water
a lemon-sized piece of tamarind pulp
1 cup (8 fl oz) hot water
1 cup chopped mixed vegetables
(e.g. radish, onion, okra [lady's fingers], eggplant
(aubergine), sweet pepper (capsicum), potato, drumstick)
2 green chillies (chili peppers), slit sideways
1 cup (8 fl oz) water
salt to taste
½ teaspoon ground turmeric
3 teaspoons sambar powder (see Sambar Powder 2, p. 136)
1 tablespoon rice flour (optional)
2 tablespoons extra water (optional)
1 small bunch of coriander (Chinese parsley) leaves,
chopped (to garnish)*

FOR TEMPERING

*1–1½ tablespoons oil
1 teaspoon brown mustard seeds
½ teaspoon asafoetida powder
½ teaspoon fenugreek seeds
½ teaspoon cumin seeds
1 red chilli (chili pepper), halved
a few curry leaves*

Method

Wash red gram dal well. Drain. Place dal in a heavy saucepan. Cover with 2 cups (16 fl oz) water and bring to the boil. When boiling, cover pan with a lid, leaving slightly ajar. Lower the heat, and simmer dal gently for 1½ hours. Stir several times during the last 30 minutes of cooking. Set dal aside without draining.

Soak the tamarind in 1 cup (8 fl oz) hot water for 15 minutes. Strain the tamarind water into another container, squeezing as much liquid as possible out of the tamarind pulp. Discard the pulp. Set the juice aside.

Select enough vegetables to fill approx. 1 cup when chopped. Peel and prepare as necessary. Chop into 1 cm (½ in) pieces. Set aside.

TEMPERING: Heat 1½ tablespoons oil in a heavy saucepan. Add the mustard seeds, asafoetida powder, fenugreek seeds, cumin seeds, halved red chilli, and a few curry leaves.

When the mustard seeds splutter, add the slit green chillies and chopped vegetables. Sauté for a couple of minutes. Add tamarind juice, 1 cup (8 fl oz) water, salt to taste, ground turmeric, and sambar powder. Cover and simmer over a low heat until the vegetables are tender. Add the undrained cooked dal. Simmer for 5 minutes, until thoroughly blended. If the sambar needs to be thickened, make a smooth paste of the rice flour in 2 tablespoons extra water. Add to the sambar and cook for 2–3 minutes.

Garnish with the chopped coriander leaves. Serve hot with rice.

For a more distinctive flavour, use only one type of vegetable. When using drumstick by itself, cut it into pieces 5–8 cm (2–3 in) long.

Adjust the amount of oil added while tempering. Vegetables such as onion, okra etc will require a little more oil.

SMALL ONION SAMBAR
Vengaya Sambar

PREPARATION TIME: 45 MIN. COOKING TIME: 2 HRS
SERVES 4

*½ cup (3 oz) red gram dal (pigeon peas, toor dal),
picked over and rinsed
2 cups (16 fl oz) water
a lemon-sized piece of tamarind pulp
1½ cups (12 fl oz) hot water
½ teaspoon ground turmeric
salt to taste
1 bunch of coriander (Chinese parsley) leaves,
finely chopped (to garnish)*

MASALA PASTE

*2 teaspoons oil
½ teaspoon fenugreek seeds
6 red chillies (chili peppers)
½ teaspoon asafoetida powder
1 teaspoon cumin seeds
3 tablespoons coriander seeds
1½ tablespoons Bengal gram dal
(yellow split peas, chana dal), picked over and rinsed*

OPPOSITE – *Ordinary Sambar (top left)
and Small Onion Sambar (bottom right)*

2 teaspoons poppy seeds
3–4 tablespoons grated fresh coconut or
4–5 tablespoons flaked coconut
250 g (8 oz) golden shallots, peeled*
a little water

FOR TEMPERING

2 tablespoons oil
1 teaspoon brown mustard seeds
1 teaspoon cumin seeds
¼ teaspoon fenugreek seeds
1 red chilli (chili pepper), halved
a few curry leaves

Method

Rinse red gram dal well. Place in a heavy saucepan. Cover with 2 cups (16 fl oz) water and bring to the boil. When boiling, cover pan, leaving the lid slightly ajar. Lower heat, and simmer gently for 1½ hours. Stir several times during the last 30 minutes of cooking. Set dal aside without draining.

Soak the tamarind in 1½ cups (12 fl oz) hot water for 15 minutes. Strain tamarind water into another container, squeezing as much liquid as possible out of the pulp. Discard pulp. Set the juice aside.

MASALA PASTE: Heat 2 teaspoons oil in a heavy frying pan or skillet. Add fenugreek seeds, 6 red chillies, asafoetida powder, cumin seeds, coriander seeds, Bengal gram dal, and poppy seeds. Sauté for 2–3 minutes. Blend to a fine paste in an electric blender or food processor with the grated coconut, 4–6 of the peeled shallots, roughly chopped (reserve the remaining shallots), and very little water. Set aside.

TEMPERING: Heat 2 tablespoons oil in a heavy saucepan. Add the mustard seeds, cumin seeds, fenugreek seeds, halved red chilli, and a few curry leaves.

When the mustard seeds splutter, add remaining whole shallots. Sauté over a low heat for about 5 minutes. Add tamarind juice, ground turmeric, and salt to taste. Cover and simmer for 5–7 minutes until the raw smell of tamarind disappears. Add undrained cooked dal and masala paste. Cook for another 5 minutes, until thoroughly blended. If the sambar is too thick, add ¼ cup (2 fl oz) water and bring to the boil. Garnish with the finely chopped coriander leaves.

Serve hot with rice.

* Golden shallots are often referred to as sambar onions in South India. (You can use spring onions or scallions instead.) Add eggplants (aubergines) and drumsticks to the shallots, for extra flavour. This sambar goes well with dosais and idlis, particularly Masala Dosai (see p. 87).

MIXED VEGETABLE COCONUT SAMBAR
Araitha Sambar

PREPARATION TIME: 30 MIN. COOKING TIME: 2 HRS
SERVES 4

½ cup (3 oz) red gram dal (pigeon peas, toor dal),
picked over and rinsed
2 cups (16 fl oz) water
a lemon-sized piece of tamarind pulp
1½ cups (12 fl oz) hot water
1 small eggplant (aubergine), chopped
1 sweet pepper (capsicum), chopped
drumstick, chopped
1 small potato, quartered
½ cup (approx. 4 oz) golden shallots, peeled and chopped*
salt to taste
½ teaspoon ground turmeric
1 small bunch of coriander (Chinese parsley) leaves,
finely chopped (to garnish)

PASTE

2 teaspoons oil
½ teaspoon fenugreek seeds
6 red chillies (chili peppers)
½ teaspoon asafoetida powder
1 teaspoon cumin seeds
3 tablespoons coriander seeds
1½ tablespoons Bengal gram dal
(yellow split peas, chana dal), picked over and rinsed
3–4 tablespoons grated fresh coconut or
4–5 tablespoons flaked coconut
a little water

FOR TEMPERING

2 tablespoons oil
1 teaspoon brown mustard seeds
1 teaspoon cumin seeds
¼ teaspoon fenugreek seeds
1 red chilli (chili pepper), halved
a few curry leaves

OPPOSITE – *Mixed Vegetable Coconut Sambar*

Method

Wash the red gram dal well. Drain. Place dal in a heavy saucepan. Cover with 2 cups (16 fl oz) water and bring to the boil. When boiling, cover pan with a lid, leaving slightly ajar. Lower heat, and simmer the dal gently for 1½ hours. Stir several times during the last 30 minutes of cooking. Set dal aside without draining.

Soak the tamarind in 1½ cups (12 fl oz) hot water for 15 minutes. Strain the tamarind water into another container, squeezing as much liquid as possible out of the tamarind pulp. Discard the pulp. Set the juice aside.

PASTE: Heat 2 teaspoons oil in a heavy frying pan or skillet. Add the fenugreek seeds, red chillies, asafoetida powder, cumin seeds, coriander seeds, and Bengal gram dal. Sauté for 2–3 minutes. Remove from the heat and place mixture in an electric blender or food processor. Add the grated coconut and just a little water. Blend ingredients to a fine paste. Set aside.

Chop the eggplant and sweet pepper into 1 cm (½ in) pieces. Chop the drumstick into 5 cm (2 in) lengths. Peel and quarter the potato. Set the vegetables aside.

TEMPERING: Heat 2 tablespoons oil in a heavy saucepan. Add the mustard seeds, cumin seeds, fenugreek seeds, halved red chilli, and a few curry leaves.

When the mustard seeds splutter, add the chopped shallots and sauté for 1 minute. Add all the chopped vegetables, tamarind juice, salt to taste, and ground turmeric. Cover pan and simmer for 10 minutes, until the vegetables are done and the raw smell of the tamarind disappears. Add the undrained cooked dal and the paste. Cook for another 5 minutes, until thoroughly blended. If the sambar is too thick, add ¼ cup (2 fl oz) water and bring to the boil.

Garnish with the finely chopped coriander leaves. Serve hot with rice.

* If you cannot buy shallots, use spring onions or scallions instead.

BUTTERMILK SAMBAR 1

Moru Kuzhambu 1

PREPARATION TIME: 1 HOUR; COOKING TIME: 30 MIN.
SERVES 4

*1 teaspoon red gram dal (pigeon peas, toor dal),
picked over and rinsed
1 teaspoon Bengal gram dal (yellow split peas,
chana dal), picked over and rinsed
½ cup (4 fl oz) water
a piece of fresh ginger (1 cm/½ in long), finely shredded
2 teaspoons cumin seeds
1 tablespoon coriander seeds
6 green chillies (chili peppers)
3 tablespoons grated fresh coconut or
4 tablespoons flaked coconut
a little water
2 cups (16 fl oz) plain yogurt (see p. 136)
salt to taste
½ teaspoon ground turmeric
1 cup chopped ash gourd*

FOR TEMPERING

*2 teaspoons oil
1 teaspoon brown mustard seeds
1 teaspoon fenugreek seeds
1 red chilli (chili pepper), halved
½ teaspoon asafoetida powder
a few curry leaves*

Method

Soak the red gram dal and Bengal gram dal in ½ cup (4 fl oz) water for 1 hour. Drain off water.

Place the soaked dals, ginger, cumin seeds, coriander seeds, green chillies, and grated coconut in an electric blender or food processor. Add very little water and blend the ingredients to a fine paste.

Place the yogurt in a bowl. Add the ground paste, salt to taste, and ground turmeric. Mix well and set aside.

Chop the ash gourd into 1 cm (½ in) pieces. Set aside.

TEMPERING: Heat 2 teaspoons oil in a heavy saucepan. Add mustard seeds, fenugreek seeds, halved red chilli, asafoetida powder, and a few curry leaves.

When the mustard seeds splutter, add the chopped ash gourd to the pan. Pour in just enough water to cover the gourd. Cover

pan, and simmer on a low heat until cooked. Now add the yogurt mixture and heat the sambar through gently. Take particular care to prevent curdling.

Serve hot with rice.

You can make this sambar with any vegetable of your choice: e.g. okra (lady's fingers); eggplant (aubergine); sweet peppers (capsicum); or cooked diced potato. Lentil dumplings can also be used instead of vegetables. For preparation of dumplings, see p. 13.

For a slightly different flavour, use ¼–½ cup (2–4 fl oz) coconut milk instead of grated or flaked coconut. Use 8–10 tablespoons coconut to make thick coconut milk (see pp. 158–9). Blend or process the paste without the coconut and make the sambar the same way. Just before serving, add the coconut milk and stir to blend well.

BUTTERMILK SAMBAR 2

Moru Kuzhambu 2

PREPARATION TIME: 20 MIN. COOKING TIME: 25 MIN.
SERVES 4

*2 cups (16 fl oz) plain yogurt (see p. 136)
¼ teaspoon ground turmeric
salt to taste
¾ cup chopped ash gourd*

PASTE

*2 teaspoons oil
1¼ teaspoons fenugreek seeds
1¼ teaspoons black gram dal (washed urad dal),
picked over and rinsed
1 teaspoon coriander seeds
1½ tablespoons red gram dal (pigeon peas, toor dal),
picked over and rinsed
6 red chillies (chili peppers)
½ teaspoon asafoetida powder
3 tablespoons grated fresh coconut or
4 tablespoons flaked coconut
a piece of fresh ginger (1 cm/½ in long)
a little water*

FOR TEMPERING

*2 teaspoons oil
1 teaspoon brown mustard seeds
½ teaspoon fenugreek seeds*

1 teaspoon cumin seeds
1 red chilli (chili pepper), halved
a few curry leaves

Method

PASTE: Heat 2 teaspoons oil in a heavy frying pan or skillet. Add the fenugreek seeds, black gram dal, coriander seeds, red gram dal, red chillies, and asafoetida powder. Sauté for 2–3 minutes. Place the mixture in an electric blender or food processor, adding the grated coconut and ginger. Adding only very little water, blend the ingredients to a fine paste.

To the paste, add yogurt, ground turmeric, and salt to taste. Beat until the mixture is smooth. Set aside.

Chop the ash gourd into 1 cm (½ in) pieces. Set aside.

TEMPERING: Heat 2 teaspoons oil in a heavy saucepan. Add the mustard seeds, fenugreek seeds, cumin seeds, halved red chilli, and a few curry leaves.

When the mustard seeds splutter, add the chopped ash gourd and sauté for 1 minute. Add enough water to just cover the gourd, cover pan, and simmer over a low heat until the ash gourd is tender. Now add the yogurt mixture to the sambar, and heat through gently over a low heat. Remove from the heat when the sambar just begins to boil. Take care to prevent curdling.

Serve hot with rice.

This sambar also tastes delicious when made with other vegetables. Try it with okra (lady's fingers); eggplant (aubergine); sweet peppers (capsicum); green peas; or boiled, skinned and diced colocasia or potatoes.

Pepper Sambar
Milagu Kuzhambu

PREPARATION TIME: 20 MIN. COOKING TIME: 20 MIN.
SERVES 4

a large, lemon-sized piece of tamarind pulp
2 cups (16 fl oz) hot water
salt to taste
2 tablespoons sesame oil
a few curry leaves, chopped

MASALA PASTE

1¼ tablespoons black peppercorns
1¼ tablespoons Bengal gram dal (yellow split peas,
chana dal), picked over and rinsed
1 teaspoon coriander seeds
2 red chillies (chili peppers)
½ teaspoon asafoetida powder
a little water

FOR TEMPERING

2 teaspoons sesame oil
1 teaspoon brown mustard seeds

Method

Soak the tamarind in 2 cups (16 fl oz) hot water for 15 minutes. Strain the tamarind water into another container, squeezing as much liquid as possible out of the tamarind pulp. Discard pulp. Set the juice aside.

MASALA PASTE: Place the black peppercorns, Bengal gram dal, coriander seeds, red chillies, and asafoetida powder in a heavy frying pan or skillet. Heat the spices through gently for 2–3 minutes, or until they become fragrant. Blend into a fine powder using an electric blender or food processor. Now add just enough water to make a smooth paste. Set aside.

TEMPERING: Heat 2 teaspoons sesame oil in a heavy saucepan. Add the mustard seeds.

When the mustard seeds splutter, add the tamarind juice and salt to taste. Cover and simmer over a low heat for at least 10 minutes. Add the masala paste and bring sambar to the boil. Just before turning off the heat, add 2 tablespoons sesame oil and the chopped curry leaves. Serve hot with rice.

This is a fiery sambar. Mix it with a greater quantity of rice than usual, and ¼–½ teaspoon ghee or oil.

Curry Leaf Sambar
Karivepilai Kuzhambu

PREPARATION TIME: 15 MIN. COOKING TIME: 15 MIN.
SERVES 4

PASTE

5–6 red chillies (chili peppers)
1 teaspoon black peppercorns
1 teaspoon asafoetida powder
2 teaspoons black gram dal (washed urad dal),
picked over and rinsed
1½ teaspoons uncooked rice
approx. 30 curry leaves
a lemon-sized piece of tamarind pulp
a little water
2 cups (16 fl oz) water (extra)
salt to taste

FOR TEMPERING

2 tablespoons sesame oil
1 teaspoon brown mustard seeds
¼ teaspoon fenugreek seeds
1 red chilli (chili pepper), halved

Method

PASTE: Place the red chillies, black peppercorns, asafoetida powder, black gram dal, and rice in a heavy frying pan or skillet. Heat through gently until the spieces become fragrant, about 2–3 minutes. Place in an electric blender or food processor. Add curry leaves, tamarind pulp, and very little water. Blend to a fine paste.

Dissolve the paste in 2 cups (16 fl oz) water. Add salt to taste, and set aside.

TEMPERING: Heat 2 tablespoons sesame oil in a heavy saucepan. Add the mustard seeds, fenugreek seeds, and halved red chilli.

When the mustard seeds splutter, add the dissolved paste, and simmer until the sambar thickens.

Serve hot with rice and roasted poppadoms.

This thick, spicy sambar should be eaten with more rice than is usual with other sambars. Mix ¼ teaspoon of ghee or oil with the rice to help to bring out the flavour.

OPPOSITE – *Pepper Sambar (top left) and Curry Leaf Sambar (bottom right)*
PREVIOUS PAGE – *Buttermilk Sambar 1 (bottom right) and Buttermilk Sambar 2 (top left)*

SPICY TAMARIND SAMBAR
Vatral Kuzhambu

PREPARATION TIME: 15 MIN. COOKING TIME: 30 MIN.
SERVES 4

a lemon-sized piece of tamarind pulp
2 cups (16 fl oz) hot water
150 g (5 oz) golden shallots, peeled and chopped*
3 teaspoons sambar powder (see Sambar Powder 1, p. 136)
salt to taste
2 tablespoons powdered jaggery
2 tablespoons besan (chickpea flour)
1/2 cup (4 fl oz) water

FOR TEMPERING

3 tablespoons sesame oil
2 red chillies (chili peppers), halved
1 teaspoon brown mustard seeds
1/2 teaspoon asafoetida powder
1/2 teaspoon fenugreek seeds
1 teaspoon red gram dal (pigeon peas, toor dal),
picked over and rinsed
1 teaspoon Bengal gram dal (yellow split peas, chana dal),
picked over and rinsed
1 teaspoon black gram dal (washed urad dal),
a few curry leaves

Method

Soak the tamarind in 2 cups (16 fl oz) hot water for 15 minutes. Strain the tamarind water into another container, squeezing as much liquid as possible out of the tamarind pulp. Discard pulp. Set the juice aside.

TEMPERING: Heat sesame oil in a heavy saucepan. Add red chillies, mustard seeds, asafoetida powder, and fenugreek seeds. When the mustard seeds splutter, add red gram dal, Bengal gram dal, black gram dal, and a few curry leaves. Sauté until the dals turn golden.

Now add the shallots. Sauté for 2 minutes. Add sambar powder. Sauté for 1 minute. Finally, add the tamarind juice, salt to taste, and jaggery. Cover and simmer on a low heat, about 10 minutes. Meanwhile, make a batter with the besan and 1/2 cup (4 fl oz) water. Add to the sambar. Boil for 2 minutes.

Serve hot with rice.

OPPOSITE – *Mysore Sambar (bottom left)*
and Spicy Tamarind Sambar (top left)

*If you cannot get shallots, use spring onions or scallions instead. Eggplant (aubergine), sweet pepper (capsicum), or radish can also be used. Eat this tart, spicy sambar with more rice than usual, and a few drops of hot sesame oil or ghee. It can also be served with Rice Pongal (see p. 75).

MYSORE SAMBAR
Mysore Kuzhambu

PREPARATION TIME: 40 MIN. COOKING TIME: 1 HR 45 MIN.
SERVES 4

3/4 cup (5 oz) red gram dal (pigeon peas, toor dal),
picked over and rinsed
3 cups (24 fl oz) water
250 g (1 2/3 cups, 8 oz) green or string beans, chopped
1 potato, peeled and chopped
2 tablespoons shelled green peas
1/2 teaspoon ground turmeric
salt to taste

PASTE

1 tablespoon coriander seeds
1/2 fresh coconut, grated
1 teaspoon brown mustard seeds
1 tablespoon uncooked long-grained rice
6 red chillies (chili peppers)
1/2 teaspoon asafoetida powder
a little water

FOR TEMPERING

2 teaspoons oil
1 teaspoon brown mustard seeds
1 teaspoon cumin seeds
1 red chilli (chili pepper), halved
a few curry leaves

Method

Wash the red gram dal well. Drain. Place dal in a heavy saucepan. Cover with 3 cups (24 fl oz) water and bring to the boil. When boiling, cover pan with a lid, leaving slightly ajar. Lower heat, and simmer dal gently for 1 1/2 hours. Stir several times during the last 30 minutes of cooking. Set dal aside without draining.

PASTE: Place the coriander seeds, grated coconut, brown mustard seeds, uncooked rice, red chillies, and asafoetida powder in an electric blender or food processor. Adding very little water, blend ingredients to a fine paste. Set aside.

Chop beans and potato into 1 cm (½ in) pieces. Place in a saucepan with shelled peas and water to just cover. Cook until tender. Add the undrained dal, ground turmeric, salt to taste, and paste. Simmer gently, until well blended.

TEMPERING: Heat 2 teaspoons oil in a heavy frying pan or skillet. Add the mustard seeds, cumin seeds, halved red chilli, and a few curry leaves.

When the mustard seeds splutter, add the mixture to the sambar and stir thoroughly.

Serve hot with rice.

DUMPLING SAMBAR
Parupu Urundai Kuzhambu

PREPARATION TIME: 3 HRS; COOKING TIME: 30 MIN.
SERVES 4

a lemon-sized piece of tamarind pulp
2 cups (16 fl oz) hot water
3 teaspoons sambar powder (see Sambar Powder 1, p. 130)
salt to taste (extra)
2 tablespoons powdered jaggery

DUMPLINGS

1 cup (6 oz) red gram dal (pigeon peas, toor dal),
picked over and rinsed
4–6 red chillies (chili peppers)
1/2 teaspoon asafoetida powder
salt to taste
1 tablespoon oil
a few curry leaves

FOR TEMPERING

2 tablespoons sesame oil
1 teaspoon brown mustard seeds
1/2 teaspoon fenugreek seeds
2 red chillies (chili peppers), halved
1/2 teaspoon asafoetida powder
a few curry leaves
1 teaspoon black gram dal (washed urad dal),
picked over and rinsed
1 teaspoon Bengal gram dal (yellow split peas,
chana dal), picked over and rinsed
1 teaspoon red gram dal (pigeon peas, toor dal),
picked over and rinsed

Method

Soak the tamarind in 2 cups (16 fl oz) hot water for 15 minutes. Strain the tamarind water into another container, squeezing as much liquid as possible out of the tamarind pulp. Discard pulp. Set the juice aside.

DUMPLINGS: Soak the red gram dal and chillies in water for 2–3 hours. Drain. Place dal and chillies in an electric blender or food processor. Add salt to taste and asafoetida powder. Blend the ingredients to a thick paste.

Heat 1 tablespoon oil in a heavy frying pan or skillet. Add a few curry leaves and the ground paste. Sauté for 2–3 minutes.

Remove from the heat and shape mixture into small balls. Place the dumplings on an idli stand or steamer. Steam in a pressure cooker (without the weight) for about 10 minutes, or in a saucepan for about 20 minutes. Set aside and allow to cool.

TEMPERING: Heat the oil in a heavy saucepan. Add mustard seeds, fenugreek seeds, red chillies, asafoetida powder, and a few curry leaves. When the mustard seeds splutter, add the black gram dal, Bengal gram dal, and red gram dal. Sauté until golden.

Add the sambar powder. Sauté for 1 minute. Now add tamarind juice, salt to taste, and jaggery. Cover and simmer for 10 minutes. Lastly, add the steamed dumplings. Simmer for 10 minutes longer.

Serve hot with rice.

This is a rich, spicy sambar. Mix it judiciously with rice.

For variety, add 1/2 cup (1/2 oz) fresh grated coconut (2/3 cups flaked coconut), and chopped mung bean (moong dal) sprouts to the dumplings before you shape into balls.

CAULIFLOWER SAMBAR
Cauliflower Poritha Kuzhambu

PREPARATION TIME: 25 MIN. COOKING TIME: 1 HR 45 MIN.
SERVES 4

1/2 cup (3 oz) red gram dal (pigeon peas, toor dal),
picked over and rinsed
2 cups (16 fl oz) water
2 teaspoons rice flour
1/2 cup (4 fl oz) water (extra)
2 cups (22 oz) chopped cauliflower
(1 medium-sized cauliflower)
2 tomatoes, quartered
1 1/2 teaspoons sambar powder
(see Sambar Powder 2, p. 130)
1/2 teaspoon ground turmeric
salt to taste

PASTE

1 teaspoon oil
1 teaspoon coriander seeds
1/2 teaspoon black peppercorns
1 teaspoon black gram dal (washed urad dal),
picked over and rinsed
1/2 teaspoon asafoetida powder
1/2 fresh coconut for grating
a little water

2 teaspoons ghee
1 teaspoon brown mustard seeds
1 teaspoon black gram dal (washed urad dal),
picked over and rinsed
1 red chilli (chili pepper), halved
a few curry leaves

Method

Wash the red gram dal well. Drain. Place dal in a heavy saucepan. Cover with 2 cups (16 fl oz) water and bring to the boil. When boiling, cover pan with a lid, leaving slightly ajar. Lower heat, and simmer dal gently for 1½ hours. Stir several times during the last 30 minutes of cooking. Set dal aside without draining.

PASTE: Heat 1 teaspoon oil in a heavy frying pan or skillet. Add the coriander seeds, black peppercorns, black gram dal, and asafoetida powder. Sauté for 2 minutes. Remove from the heat. Place the mixture in an electric blender or food processor.

Grate the fresh coconut into a large bowl. Take 2 tablespoons coconut and add it to the blender. Set the rest aside. Adding only very little water, blend ingredients to a fine paste. Set aside.

Extract the milk from the remaining grated coconut (see pp. 158–9). Dissolve 2 teaspoons rice flour in extra water. Set both aside.

Place the cauliflower florets in a saucepan, with just enough water to cover the vegetable. Add the tomatoes, sambar powder, turmeric powder, and salt to taste. Simmer until the vegetables are tender. Now add the paste, the dissolved rice flour, and the undrained cooked dal. Simmer until thoroughly blended.

TEMPERING: Heat 2 teaspoons ghee in a heavy frying pan or skillet. Add the mustard seeds, black gram dal, halved red chilli, and a few curry leaves.

When the mustard seeds splutter, add this mixture to the sambar. Just before serving, add the coconut milk.

Serve hot with rice.

For a more traditional flavour, make this sambar with ridge gourd (club or sponge gourd, silk squash) or snake gourd. For a lighter sambar, use green gram dal (split mung beans, moong dal) instead of red gram dal.

OPPOSITE – *Mashed Green Gram Dal*
PREVIOUS PAGE – *Cauliflower Sambar (top left) and Dumpling Sambar (bottom right)*

MASHED GREEN GRAM DAL
Payatham Paruppu Masial
PREPARATION TIME: 10 MIN. COOKING TIME: 1 HR 45 MIN.
SERVES 4

1 cup (6 oz) green gram dal (split mung beans,
moong dal), picked over and rinsed
3 cups (24 fl oz) water
a lemon-sized piece of tamarind pulp
1 cup (8 fl oz) hot water
6 green chillies (chili peppers), slit sideways
½ teaspoon ground turmeric
salt to taste
1 small bunch of coriander (Chinese parsley) leaves,
finely chopped

FOR TEMPERING

2 teaspoons ghee
1 teaspoon brown mustard seeds
1 red chilli (chili pepper), halved
½ teaspoon asafoetida powder
a few curry leaves

METHOD

Wash the green gram dal well. Drain. Place dal in a heavy saucepan. Cover with 3 cups (24 fl oz) water and bring to the boil. When boiling, cover pan with a lid, leaving slightly ajar. Lower heat, and simmer dal gently for 1½ hours. Stir several times during the last 30 minutes of cooking. Set dal aside without draining.

Soak the tamarind in 1 cup (8 fl oz) hot water for 15 minutes. Strain the tamarind water into another container, squeezing as much liquid as possible out of the tamarind pulp. Discard pulp. Set the juice aside.

TEMPERING: Heat 2 teaspoons ghee in a heavy saucepan. Add the mustard seeds, halved red chilli, asafoetida powder, and a few curry leaves.

When the mustard seeds splutter, add the green chillies, tamarind juice, ground turmeric, and salt to taste. Simmer until the raw smell of the tamarind disappears.

Now add the undrained cooked dal. Simmer mixture until thoroughly blended.

Garnish with the finely chopped coriander leaves. Serve hot with rice or chapattis.

BITTER GOURD PITLAY

Paavakkai Pitlay

PREPARATION TIME: 40 MIN. COOKING TIME: 25 MIN.
SERVES 4

½ cup (3 oz) red gram dal (pigeon peas, toor dal),
picked over and rinsed
2 cups (16 fl oz) water
a lemon-sized piece of tamarind paste
1 cup (8 fl oz) hot water
6 raw cashew nuts, halved (optional)
1 tablespoon ghee (optional)
2–3 medium-sized bitter gourds
(bitter melons), finely chopped
salt to taste
2 teaspoons sambar powder
(see Sambar Powder 2, p. 136)
½ teaspoon ground turmeric
1 tablespoon powdered jaggery
1 tomato, finely chopped
2½ cups (20 fl oz) water (extra)

PASTE

2 teaspoons oil
6 red chillies (chili peppers)
1 tablespoon coriander seeds
½ teaspoon black peppercorns
1 teaspoon Bengal gram dal (yellow split peas,
chana dal), picked over and rinsed
1 teaspoon black gram dal (washed urad dal),
picked over and rinsed
½ teaspoon asafoetida powder
½ fresh coconut, grated

FOR TEMPERING

2 teaspoons oil
1 teaspoon brown mustard seeds
a few curry leaves

Method

Wash the red gram dal well. Drain. Place dal in a heavy saucepan. Cover with 2 cups (16 fl oz) water and bring to the boil. When boiling, cover pan with a lid, leaving slightly ajar. Lower heat, and simmer dal gently for 1½ hours. Stir several times during the last 30 minutes of cooking. Set dal aside without draining.

Soak the tamarind in 1 cup (8 fl oz) hot water for 15 minutes. Strain the tamarind water into another container, squeezing as much liquid as possible out of the tamarind pulp. Discard pulp. Set the juice aside.

PASTE: Heat 2 teaspoons oil in a heavy frying pan or skillet. Add the red chillies, coriander seeds, black peppercorns, Bengal gram dal, black gram dal, and asafoetida powder. Sauté for 2–3 minutes. Place mixture in an electric blender or food processor. Grate the fresh coconut into a bowl. Add 2 tablespoons coconut to the blender. Set the rest aside. Blend ingredients to a fine paste and set aside.

Extract the milk from the remaining grated coconut (see pp. 158–9). Set aside.

Sauté the cashew nuts (if used) in 1 tablespoon ghee. Set aside for garnish.

Heat the tamarind juice in a heavy saucepan. Add the finely chopped bitter gourd, salt to taste, sambar powder, ground turmeric, and jaggery. Simmer over a low heat until the bitter gourd is cooked.

Now add the finely chopped tomato and ground paste. Simmer the pitlay for 2 minutes. Add the undrained cooked dal, and continue simmering until thoroughly blended. Add extra water as needed.

TEMPERING: Heat 2 teaspoons oil in a heavy frying pan or skillet. Add the mustard seeds and a few curry leaves.

When the mustard seeds splutter, add this mixture to the pitlay. Just before serving, add the coconut milk.

Garnish with the cashew nuts. Serve hot with rice.

OPPOSITE – *Bitter Gourd Pitlay*

RASAMS

The traditional second course of a South Indian meal is the versatile thin, watery rasam — quick and easy to prepare. Tamarind, tomatoes, and lime give it a piquant tangy taste. Use the tamarind and tomatoes judiciously. If you use more tomatoes, reduce the quantity of tamarind accordingly, and vice versa. Wet rice with your rasam or eat as you would a soup.

~

Health-conscious South Indians often make a light meal of the easily digestible rasam and chutney for the evening meal, preferring it to the heavier sambar. Of course, rich and spicy rasams such as Mysore Rasam and Spicy Lentil Rasam only require soothing Curd Rice (p. 70) to complete the meal.

~

There's nothing like making your own rasam powder, but if you are hard pressed for time, use any one of the good ready-made brands available in Indian markets, spice stores, or some Asian food stores.

ORDINARY RASAM
Rasam

PREPARATION TIME: 10 MIN. COOKING TIME: 1 HR 40 MIN.
SERVES 4

3 tablespoons red gram dal (pigeon peas, toor dal),
picked over and rinsed
1 cup (8 fl oz) water
2 tomatoes, diced
a lemon-sized piece of tamarind pulp
1/2 teaspoon asafoetida powder
2 teaspoons Rasam Powder (see p. 138)
salt to taste
2 1/2 cups (20 fl oz) water (extra)
coriander (Chinese parsley) leaves, chopped (to garnish)

FOR TEMPERING

2 teaspoons ghee
1 teaspoon brown mustard seeds
1/2 teaspoon cumin seeds
1 red chilli (chili pepper), halved
a few curry leaves

Method

Wash red gram dal well. Drain. Place dal in a heavy saucepan. Cover with 1 cup (8 fl oz) water and bring to the boil. When boiling, cover pan with a lid, leaving slightly ajar. Lower the heat, and simmer dal gently for 1 1/2 hours. Stir several times during the last 30 minutes of cooking. Set dal aside without draining.

Dice the tomatoes. Place in a heavy saucepan with the tamarind pulp, asafoetida powder, rasam powder, and salt to taste. Add 1 cup (8 fl oz) water. Crush the contents of the pan together. Simmer for about 15 minutes.

Add the undrained cooked dal and the remaining 1 1/2 cups (12 fl oz) water to the rasam. Bring to the boil.

TEMPERING: Heat 2 teaspoons ghee in a heavy frying pan or skillet. Add the mustard seeds, cumin seeds, halved red chilli, and a few curry leaves.

When the mustard seeds splutter, add this mixture to the rasam.

Garnish the rasam with chopped coriander leaves. Serve hot.

OPPOSITE – *Ordinary Rasam (bottom left)*
and Tomato Rasam (top right)

TOMATO RASAM
Thakkali Rasam

PREPARATION TIME: 10 MIN. COOKING TIME: 1 HR 40 MIN.
SERVES 4

3 tablespoons red gram dal (pigeon peas,
toor dal), picked over and rinsed
1 cup (8 fl oz) water
3 green chillies (chili peppers), slit sideways
a piece of fresh ginger (2 1/2 cm/1 in), finely chopped
4 large tomatoes, finely chopped
2 1/2 cups (20 fl oz) water (extra)
salt to taste
1/2 teaspoon ground turmeric
coriander (Chinese parsley) leaves, chopped (to garnish)

FOR TEMPERING

2 teaspoons ghee
1 teaspoon brown mustard seeds
1 teaspoon cumin seeds
1 red chilli (chili pepper), halved
1 teaspoon ground black pepper
1/2 teaspoon asafoetida powder
a few curry leaves

Method

Wash red gram dal well. Drain. Place dal in a heavy saucepan. Cover with 1 cup (8 fl oz) water and bring to the boil. When boiling, cover pan with a lid, leaving slightly ajar. Lower the heat, and simmer dal gently for 1 1/2 hours. Stir several times during the last 30 minutes of cooking. Set dal aside without draining.

TEMPERING: Heat 2 teaspoons ghee in a heavy saucepan. Add the mustard seeds, cumin seeds, halved red chilli, black pepper, asafoetida powder, and a few curry leaves.

When the mustard seeds splutter, add slit green chillies, and finely chopped ginger and tomatoes. Add 1 cup (8 fl oz) water, salt to taste, and ground turmeric. Allow to simmer for 5 minutes. Add undrained cooked dal and remaining 1 1/2 cups (12 fl oz) water. Bring to the boil.

Garnish the rasam with chopped coriander leaves. Serve hot.

This is a mild, gentle rasam without tamarind and rasam powder. Add more tomatoes for a tangier taste. The strained rasam, served as a soup, makes an excellent appetiser.

LEMON RASAM
Elumichampazha Rasam

PREPARATION TIME: 20 MIN. COOKING TIME: 2 HRS
SERVES 4

$^1/_4$ cup or 4 tablespoons red gram dal (pigeon peas,
toor dal), picked over and rinsed
1 cup (8 fl oz) water
a piece of fresh ginger (2$^1/_2$ cm/1 in), peeled and grated
4 green chillies (chili peppers)
$^1/_2$ teaspoon cumin seeds
$^3/_4$ teaspoon black peppercorns
1$^1/_2$ cups (12 fl oz) water (extra)
2 tomatoes, quartered
$^1/_2$ teaspoon ground turmeric
salt to taste
juice of 1 lemon
coriander (Chinese parsley) leaves, chopped (to garnish)

FOR TEMPERING

2 teaspoons ghee
1 teaspoon brown mustard seeds
$^1/_2$ teaspoon asafoetida powder
1 red chilli (chili pepper), halved
a few curry leaves

Method

Wash red gram dal well. Drain. Place dal in a heavy saucepan. Cover with 1 cup (8 fl oz) water and bring to the boil. When boiling, cover pan with a lid, leaving slightly ajar. Lower the heat, and simmer dal gently for 1$^1/_2$ hours. Stir several times during the last 30 minutes of cooking. Set dal aside without draining.

Using an electric blender or food processor, blend the fresh ginger and green chillies into a paste. Now blend or process the cumin seeds and black peppercorns into a powder. Set both aside.

Place the undrained cooked dal in a heavy saucepan. Add 1$^1/_2$ cups (12 fl oz) extra water, quartered tomatoes, ground turmeric, salt to taste, and ginger/chilli paste. Slowly bring to the boil.

TEMPERING: Heat 2 teaspoons ghee in a heavy frying pan or skillet. Add mustard seeds, asafoetida powder, halved red chilli, a few curry leaves, and pepper/cumin seed powder.

When the mustard seeds splutter, add this mixture to the rasam. Turn off the heat and add the lemon juice.

Garnish with chopped coriander. Serve hot with rice.

GINGER RASAM
Inji Rasam

PREPARATION TIME: 35 MIN. COOKING TIME: 20 MIN.
SERVES 4

3 tablespoons red gram dal (pigeon peas, toor dal),
picked over and rinsed
1 cup (8 fl oz) water
3–4 teaspoons cumin seeds
1 teaspoon black peppercorns
3 green chillies (chili peppers)
2–3 pieces of fresh ginger (2$^1/_2$ cm/1 in)
3 teaspoons grated copra
1 tablespoon powdered jaggery
1$^1/_2$ cups (12 fl oz) water (extra)
salt to taste
coriander (Chinese parsley) leaves, chopped (to garnish)

FOR TEMPERING

2 teaspoons ghee
1 teaspoon brown mustard seeds
1 teaspoon cumin seeds
$^1/_2$ teaspoon asafoetida powder
1 red chilli (chili pepper), halved
a few curry leaves

Method

Soak the red gram dal in 1 cup (8 fl oz) water for 30 minutes. Drain off water and set, dal aside.

Place the cumin seeds, black peppercorns, green chillies, ginger, grated copra, and jaggery in an electric blender or food processor. Add the soaked dal and blend ingredients to a fine paste. Place in a heavy saucepan. Add 1$^1/_2$ cups (12 fl oz) water and salt to taste. Bring to the boil. Simmer over a low heat for 2–3 minutes. Add more water if the rasam is too thick.

TEMPERING: Heat 2 teaspoons ghee in a heavy frying pan or skillet. Add mustard seeds, cumin seeds, asafoetida powder, halved red chilli, and a few curry leaves.

When the mustard seeds splutter, add this mixture to the rasam. Garnish with chopped coriander leaves. Serve hot.

OPPOSITE – *Ginger Rasam (top)*
and Lemon Rasam (bottom)

CUMIN SEED & PEPPER RASAM
Jeera-Milagu Rasam

PREPARATION TIME: 20 MIN. COOKING TIME: 15 MIN.
SERVES 4

a lemon-sized piece of tamarind pulp
1 cup (8 fl oz) hot water
salt to taste

PASTE

1 teaspoon ghee
1½ teaspoons black peppercorns
1 teaspoon cumin seeds
1 teaspoon red gram dal (pigeon peas, toor dal),
picked over and rinsed
1 red chilli (chili pepper)
½ teaspoon asafoetida powder
a little water

FOR TEMPERING

2 teaspoons ghee
1 teaspoon brown mustard seeds
½ teaspoon cumin seeds
1 red chilli (chili pepper), halved
a few curry leaves

Method

Soak the tamarind in 1 cup (8 fl oz) hot water for 15 minutes. Strain the tamarind water into another container, squeezing as much liquid as possible out of the tamarind pulp. Discard pulp. Set the juice aside.

PASTE: Heat 1 teaspoon ghee in a heavy frying pan or skillet. Add the black peppercorns, cumin seeds, red gram dal, red chilli, and asafoetida powder. Sauté for 2–3 minutes. Blend mixture to a fine paste in an electric blender or food processor, adding a little water if necessary. Set the paste aside.

TEMPERING: Heat 2 teaspoons ghee in a heavy saucepan. Add the mustard seeds, cumin seeds, halved red chili, and a few curry leaves.

When the mustard seeds splutter, add tamarind juice and salt to taste. Simmer for a few minutes, until the raw smell disappears. Add the paste and simmer for 2 minutes only.* Serve hot with rice.

* If boiled for too long, pepper will spoil the taste of the dish.

OPPOSITE – *Cumin Seed and Pepper Rasam (bottom left) and Garlic Rasam (top right)*

GARLIC RASAM
Poondu Rasam

PREPARATION TIME: 20 MIN. COOKING TIME: 20 MIN.
SERVES 4

a lemon-sized piece of tamarind pulp
2 cups (16 fl oz) hot water
salt to taste
a few curry leaves
20–25 garlic cloves, peeled but left whole
2 teaspoons oil

PASTE

2 teaspoons oil
4 red chillies (chili peppers)
¾ teaspoon black peppercorns
2 teaspoons coriander seeds
1 teaspoon Bengal gram dal (yellow split peas,
chana dal), picked over and rinsed
1 teaspoon cumin seeds
a few curry leaves

FOR TEMPERING

2 teaspoons ghee
1 teaspoon brown mustard seeds
2 red chillies (chili peppers), halved

Method

PASTE: Heat 2 teaspoons oil in a heavy frying pan or skillet. Add the 4 red chillies, black peppercorns, coriander seeds, and Bengal gram dal. Sauté for 2–3 minutes. Place mixture in an electric blender or food processor. Add the cumin seeds and a few curry leaves. Blend ingredients to a fine paste. Set aside.

Soak the tamarind in 2 cups (16 fl oz) hot water for 15 minutes. Strain the tamarind water into another container, squeezing as much liquid as possible out of the tamarind pulp. Discard pulp. Place juice in a heavy saucepan. Add the salt and extra curry leaves. Simmer over a low heat until the raw smell disappears.

Meanwhile, sauté the garlic cloves in 2 teaspoons oil, until golden. Add to the boiling tamarind juice with the paste. Simmer until well blended. Add more water if the rasam is too thick.

TEMPERING: Heat 2 teaspoons ghee in a heavy frying pan or skillet. Add the mustard seeds and halved red chillies.

When the mustard seeds splutter, add this mixture to the rasam. Serve hot.

BUTTERMILK RASAM
Moru Rasam

PREPARATION TIME: 20 MIN. COOKING TIME: 2 HRS
SERVES 4

¼ cup or 4 tablespoons red gram dal (pigeon peas,
toor dal), picked over and rinsed
1 cup (8 fl oz) water
1 cup (8 fl oz) water (extra)
1 tomato, quartered
salt to taste
1 cup (8 fl oz) buttermilk

PASTE

2 teaspoons ghee
4 red chillies (chili peppers)
1 teaspoon coriander seeds
1 teaspoon red gram dal (pigeon peas, toor dal),
picked over and rinsed
¼ teaspoon fenugreek seeds
¼ teaspoon black peppercorns
½ teaspoon asafoetida powder
a little water

FOR TEMPERING

2 teaspoons ghee
1 teaspoon brown mustard seeds
1 teaspoon cumin seeds
1 red chilli (chili pepper), halved
a few curry leaves

Method

Wash red gram dal well. Drain. Place dal in a heavy saucepan. Cover with 1 cup (8 fl oz) water and bring to the boil. When boiling, cover pan with a lid, leaving slightly ajar. Lower the heat, and simmer dal gently for 1½ hours. Stir several times during the last 30 minutes of cooking. Set dal aside without draining.

PASTE: Heat 2 teaspoons ghee in a heavy frying pan or skillet. Add the 4 red chillies, coriander seeds, red gram dal, fenugreek seeds, black peppercorns, and asafoetida powder. Sauté for 2–3 minutes. Place mixture in an electric blender or food processor. Blend ingredients to a fine paste, adding very little water. Set aside.

Place the undrained cooked dal in a heavy saucepan. Add 1 cup (8 fl oz) extra water, quartered tomato, and salt to taste.

Simmer until the tomato is cooked. Add the paste, and simmer the rasam for 2–3 minutes.

TEMPERING: Heat 2 teaspoons ghee in a heavy frying pan or skillet. Add the mustard seeds, cumin seeds, halved red chilli, and a few curry leaves.

When the mustard seeds splutter, add this mixture to the rasam. Remove from the heat and add the buttermilk. Mix thoroughly.

Serve the rasam hot with rice.

DRUMSTICK RASAM
Murungaikkai Rasam

PREPARATION TIME: 25 MIN. COOKING TIME: 1 HR 50 MIN.
SERVES 4

⅓ cup (2 oz) red gram dal (pigeon peas, toor dal),
picked over and rinsed
1½ cups (12 fl oz) water
4–5 drumsticks*
a lemon-sized piece of tamarind pulp
1 cup (8 fl oz) hot water
salt to taste
½ teaspoon ground turmeric
1 small bunch of coriander (Chinese parsley) leaves,
finely chopped

PASTE

2 teaspoons oil
4 red chillies (chili peppers)
½ teaspoon asafoetida powder
1 teaspoon coriander seeds
1 teaspoon black peppercorns
1½ teaspoons Bengal gram dal (yellow split peas,
chana dal), picked over and rinsed
2 tablespoons grated fresh coconut or
2½ tablespoons flaked coconut
a little water

FOR TEMPERING

2 teaspoons ghee
1 teaspoon brown mustard seeds
1 teaspoon cumin seeds
1 red chilli (chili pepper), halved
a few curry leaves

Method

Wash red gram dal well. Drain. Place dal in a heavy saucepan. Cover with 1½ cups (12 fl oz) water and bring to the boil. When boiling, cover pan with a lid, leaving slightly ajar. Lower the heat, and simmer dal gently for 1½ hours. Stir several times during the last 30 minutes of cooking. Set dal aside without draining.

PASTE: Heat 2 teaspoons oil in a heavy frying pan or skillet. Add red chillies, asafoetida powder, coriander seeds, black peppercorns, and Bengal gram dal. Sauté for 2–3 minutes. Place in an electric blender or food processor. Add the grated coconut and a little water. Blend ingredients to a fine paste. Set aside.

Scrape the drumstick kernels. Place drumsticks in a saucepan with just enough water to cover. Boil until just tender. Reserve the cooking water.** Set both aside.

Soak the tamarind in 1 cup (8 fl oz) hot water for 15 minutes. Strain the tamarind water into another container, squeezing as much liquid as possible out of the tamarind pulp. Discard pulp. Pour tamarind juice into a heavy saucepan. Add salt to taste and ground turmeric. Now add the boiled drumstick. Simmer until the raw smell of the tamarind disappears. Now add the paste and undrained cooked dal. Add more water if the rasam is too thick. Simmer until thoroughly blended.

TEMPERING: Heat 2 teaspoons ghee in a heavy frying pan or skillet. Add the mustard seeds, cumin seeds, halved red chilli, and a few curry leaves.

When the mustard seeds splutter, add this mixture to the rasam.

Garnish with the finely chopped coriander leaves. Serve hot with rice.

* If you are unable to buy fresh drumsticks, they are available canned from Asian food stores or Indian markets. Alternatively use bamboo shoots, or even celery — with a different flavour resulting, of course. Another alternative is to use 100 g (3 oz) eggplant (aubergine) in place of the drumsticks.

** Do not throw away the water in which you have boiled the drumsticks. Boil it along with the tamarind juice if necessary.

SPICY LENTIL RASAM
Poritha Rasam

PREPARATION TIME: 25 MIN. COOKING TIME: 1 HR 50 MIN.
SERVES 4

1/2 cup (3 oz) red gram dal (pigeon peas,
toor dal), picked over and rinsed
2 cups (16 fl oz) water
1/4 cup or 4 tablespoons green gram dal
(split mung beans, moong dal), picked over and rinsed
1 cup (8 fl oz) water
1 tomato, chopped
a pinch of ground turmeric
salt to taste
2 cups (16 fl oz) water (extra)
juice of 1 lemon
1 bunch of coriander (Chinese parsley)
leaves, finely chopped

PASTE

2 teaspoons oil
1 tablespoon coriander seeds
1 teaspoon cumin seeds
1 teaspoon black peppercorns
1 red chilli (chili pepper)
2 teaspoons black gram dal (washed urad dal)
1/2 teaspoon asafoetida powder
3 tablespoons grated fresh coconut or
4 tablespoons flaked coconut
a few curry leaves
a little water

FOR TEMPERING

2 teaspoons ghee
1 teaspoon brown mustard seeds
1 teaspoon cumin seeds
1 red chilli (chili pepper), halved
a few curry leaves (extra)

Method

Wash red gram dal well. Drain. Place in a heavy saucepan. Cover with 2 cups (16 fl oz) water and bring to the boil. When boiling, cover pan, leaving lid slightly ajar. Lower heat, and simmer gently for 1½ hours. Stir several times during the last 30 minutes of cooking. Set aside without draining. At the same time, wash green gram dal well. Drain. Place in a separate saucepan, add 1 cup (8 fl oz) water. Cook as for red gram dal. Do not drain.

PASTE: Heat 2 teaspoons oil in a heavy frying pan or skillet. Add the coriander seeds, cumin seeds, black peppercorns, red chilli, black gram dal, and asafoetida powder. Sauté for 2–3 minutes. Place in an electric blender or food processor. Add the grated coconut and a few curry leaves. Blend ingredients to a fine paste, adding very little water. Set the paste aside.

TEMPERING: Heat 2 teaspoons ghee in a heavy saucepan. Add the mustard seeds, cumin seeds, halved red chilli, and extra curry leaves.

When the mustard seeds splutter, add the undrained cooked dals, tomato, ground turmeric, salt to taste, and 2 cups (16 fl oz) water. Simmer for a few minutes. Now add the paste. Simmer for 5 more minutes, until well blended. Remove from the heat and add the lemon juice.

Garnish with the coriander leaves. Serve hot with rice.

MYSORE RASAM

PREPARATION TIME: 20 MIN. COOKING TIME: 1 HR 35 MIN.
SERVES 4

1/2 cup (3 oz) red gram dal (pigeon peas, toor dal),
picked over and rinsed
2 cups (16 fl oz) water
a marble-sized piece of tamarind pulp
1 cup (8 fl oz) hot water
6 tablespoons grated fresh coconut or
8 tablespoons flaked coconut
1½ cups (12 fl oz) hot water (extra)
3–4 small tomatoes, quartered
3 teaspoons Mysore Rasam Powder (see p. 139)
salt to taste
1/4 teaspoon ground turmeric
2 tablespoons powdered jaggery
1 small bunch of coriander
(Chinese parsley) leaves, chopped

FOR TEMPERING

1 tablespoon ghee
1 teaspoon brown mustard seeds
1 teaspoon cumin seeds
1 red chilli (chili pepper), halved
1/2 teaspoon asafoetida powder
a few curry leaves

Method

Wash red gram dal well. Drain. Place in a heavy saucepan. Cover with 2 cups (16 fl oz) water and bring to the boil. When boiling, cover pan, leaving lid slightly ajar. Lower heat and simmer gently for 1½ hours. Stir several times during the last 30 minutes of cooking. Set dal aside without draining.

Soak the tamarind in 1 cup (8 fl oz) hot water for 15 minutes. Strain tamarind water into another container, squeezing as much liquid as possible out of the tamarind pulp. Discard pulp and set juice aside. Soak the grated coconut in the hot water and extract the milk (see pp. 158–9). Set aside.

TEMPERING: Heat 1 tablespoon ghee in a heavy saucepan. Add the mustard seeds, cumin seeds, halved red chilli, asafoetida powder, and a few curry leaves.

When the mustard seeds splutter, add the quartered tomatoes, tamarind juice, Mysore Rasam Powder, salt to taste, ground turmeric, and jaggery. Simmer over a low heat for 15–20 minutes.

Add the undrained cooked dal. Simmer for 5 minutes longer, until thoroughly blended. Just before serving, add the coconut milk and chopped coriander leaves.

Serve the rasam hot with rice and poppadoms.

ABOVE – *Mysore Rasam (bottom left) and Spicy Lentil Rasam (top right)*
PREVIOUS PAGE – *Drumstick Rasam (bottom left) and Buttermilk Rasam (top right)*

PORIYALS
& KOOTUS

Poriyals, also known as dry curries, have no sauce and make a perfect accompaniment to any course. Beautifully balanced, with a subtle blending of flavours, poriyals add freshness and a wholesome goodness to any meal. The vegetables are stir-fried gently over a low heat, steamed, or boiled lightly in their natural juices so that they retain their colour and the basic aroma of the fresh vegetable. In a few poriyals, the vegetables are deep-fried, and are delightfully crisp and spicy.

~

Not quite a poriyal, not quite a sambar, the versatile kootus are neither too wet nor too dry. Just right, in fact, to be mixed with rice or eaten as a side dish. In most South Indian homes, they make do without a sambar if a kootu is part of the meal. Some South Indians eat their kootus with chapattis. Kootus are the ideal choice if you feel like a less spicy meal.

Bean Poriyal

PREPARATION TIME: 15 MIN. COOKING TIME: 10 MIN.
SERVES 4

500 g (1 lb) green or string beans, finely chopped
2 tablespoons grated coconut or
2½ tablespoons flaked coconut
salt to taste
2 tablespoons water

FOR TEMPERING

2 teaspoons oil
1 teaspoon brown mustard seeds
1 teaspoon cumin seeds
1 teaspoon black gram dal (washed urad dal),
picked over and rinsed
1 teaspoon Bengal gram dal (yellow split peas,
chana dal), picked over and rinsed
1 red chilli (chili pepper), halved
½ teaspoon asafoetida powder
a few curry leaves

Method

Trim the ends of the beans if necessary. Chop the beans finely and set aside. If using fresh coconut, grate and set aside.

TEMPERING: Heat 2 teaspoons oil in a heavy saucepan. Add the mustard seeds, cumin seeds, black gram dal, Bengal gram dal, halved red chilli, asafoetida powder, and a few curry leaves.

When the mustard seeds splutter, add the chopped beans, salt to taste, and 2 tablespoons water. Cover saucepan with a lid and simmer over a low heat until the beans are tender. Add the grated coconut. Mix thoroughly.

Serve hot.

In South India, cluster beans are often used instead of green beans. Fresh shelled peas made the same way also taste delicious. Or try this recipe with whatever fresh bean is in season. Broad or fava beans can also be cooked in this way.

Sweet Pepper Poriyal
Kudamilagai Poriyal

PREPARATION TIME: 20 MIN. COOKING TIME: 15 MIN.
SERVES 4

500 g (1 lb) sweet peppers (capsicum), chopped
2 tablespoons plain yogurt (see p. 136)
2 tablespoons water
salt to taste
2 teaspoons curry powder (see p. 139) (optional)

FOR TEMPERING

3 teaspoons oil
1 teaspoon brown mustard seeds
1 teaspoon cumin seeds
½ teaspoon asafoetida powder
a few curry leaves

Method

Chop the sweet peppers into 1 cm (½ in) pieces. Place in a bowl. Add the 2 tablespoons yogurt and smear over the chopped peppers. Set aside for 10 minutes.

TEMPERING: Heat 3 teaspoons oil in a heavy saucepan. Add the mustard seeds, cumin seeds, asafoetida powder, and a few curry leaves.

When the mustard seeds splutter, add the chopped peppers, 2 tablespoons water, and salt to taste. Cover saucepan with a lid and simmer until tender. Sprinkle over the curry powder (if used). Stir thoroughly and cook for a few more minutes.

Serve hot.

To add variety, toss a few pieces of diced potato through the sweet peppers.

If fresh gherkins are available, cook them the same way, but without smearing with yogurt.

OPPOSITE – *Bean Poriyal (top) and Sweet Poriyal (bottom)*

YAM PORIYAL
Chenaikizhangu Poriyal

PREPARATION TIME: 30 MIN. COOKING TIME: 25 MIN.
SERVES 4

500 g (1 lb) yam*
salt to taste
½ teaspoon ground turmeric
2 green chillies (chili peppers), slit sideways
2 tablespoons grated fresh coconut
or 2½ tablespoons flaked coconut
3 teaspoons curry powder (see p. 139)

FOR TEMPERING

2 teaspoons oil
1 teaspoon brown mustard seeds
1 teaspoon black gram dal (washed urad dal),
picked over and rinsed
1 teaspoon Bengal gram dal (yellow split peas,
chana dal), picked over and rinsed
1 red chilli (chili pepper), halved
½ teaspoon asafoetida powder
a few curry leaves

Method

Peel the yam and chop finely. Wash well. Add the salt to taste and ground turmeric. Mix thoroughly. Pressure cook without adding water to the yam, or steam for 20–25 minutes until cooked. Drain yam in a colander and allow to cool completely. Set aside.

TEMPERING: Heat the oil in a heavy saucepan. Add mustard seeds, black gram dal, Bengal gram dal, halved red chilli, asafoetida powder, and a few curry leaves.

When the mustard seeds splutter, add the slit green chillies and the cooked yam. Stir thoroughly. Now add the grated coconut and curry powder. Mix thoroughly and heat the poriyal through gently. Serve hot.

* If yams are unavailable, potatoes, sweet potato, or kumara, may be substituted — with a slightly different flavour resulting, of course.

CABBAGE PORIYAL
Muttakos Poriyal

PREPARATION TIME: 20 MIN. COOKING TIME: 10 MIN.
SERVES 4

2 green chillies (chili peppers), slit sideways
500 g (1 lb) cabbage, finely chopped
1/2 cup shelled (8 oz unshelled) green peas (optional)
salt to taste
2 tablespoons water
2 tablespoons grated fresh coconut or
2 1/2 tablespoons flaked coconut

FOR TEMPERING

2 teaspoons oil
1 teaspoon brown mustard seeds
1 teaspoon cumin seeds
1 teaspoon black gram dal (washed urad dal),
picked over and rinsed
1 teaspoon Bengal gram dal (yellow split peas,
chana dal), picked over and rinsed
1 red chilli (chili pepper), halved
1/2 teaspoon asafoetida powder
a few curry leaves

Method

TEMPERING: Heat 2 teaspoons oil in a heavy saucepan. Add the mustard seeds, cumin seeds, black gram dal, Bengal gram dal, halved red chilli, asafoetida powder, and a few curry leaves.

When the mustard seeds splutter, add the slit green chillies. Stir for a few seconds. Now add the finely chopped cabbage, green peas (if used), salt to taste, and 2 tablespoons water. Cover saucepan with a lid, and cook over a low heat until the vegetables are tender. Add the grated coconut. Mix thoroughly.

Serve hot.

For a spicy cabbage poriyal, make a paste of 2 green chillies, 3 tablespoons grated fresh coconut (4 tablespoons flaked coconut), 1 teaspoon cumin seeds, and a small onion. Add the cooked cabbage in place of the grated coconut.

This basic recipe may be used for almost any vegetable — carrot, choko (chayote), beetroot (beet), cauliflower, etc. Try these variations and choose your favourite.

For Cauliflower Poriyal, follow the same method as above, but do not garnish with the grated coconut.

PLANTAIN STEM PORIYAL
Vazhaithandu Poriyal

PREPARATION TIME: 1 HOUR; COOKING TIME: 20 MIN.
SERVES 4

1/4 cup or 4 tablespoons green gram dal (split mung beans,
moong dal), picked over and rinsed
1 cup (8 fl oz) water
1 plantain stem (30 cm/12 in long), finely chopped
3 cups (24 fl oz) buttermilk
2 green chillies (chili peppers), slit sideways
salt to taste
2 teaspoons sugar
1 cup (8 fl oz) water (extra)
3 tablespoons grated fresh coconut or
4 tablespoons flaked coconut

FOR TEMPERING

2 teaspoons oil
1 teaspoon brown mustard seeds
1 teaspoon cumin seeds
1 teaspoon black gram dal (washed urad dal),
picked over and rinsed
1 teaspoon Bengal gram dal (yellow split peas,
chana dal), picked over and rinsed
1 red chilli (chili pepper), halved
1/2 teaspoon asafoetida powder
a few curry leaves

Method

Soak the green gram dal in 1 cup (8 fl oz) water for 1 hour. Drain and set aside. Soak the finely chopped plantain stem in the buttermilk.* Set aside.

TEMPERING: Heat 2 teaspoons oil in a heavy saucepan. Add the mustard seeds, cumin seeds, black gram dal, Bengal gram dal, halved red chilli, asafoetida powder, and a few curry leaves.

When the mustard seeds splutter, add the slit green chillies, soaked green gram dal, chopped plantain stem (drained of buttermilk), salt to taste, sugar, and 1 cup (8 fl oz) extra water. Cover the poriyal, and simmer over a low heat until the plantain is cooked and the water has been absorbed completely.

Add the grated coconut. Mix thoroughly. Serve hot.

OPPOSITE, CLOCKWISE FROM LEFT – *Cabbage Poriyal, Plantain Stem Poriyal, and Yam Poriyal*

* The buttermilk is used to prevent the plantain from discolouring. Always remember to drain the buttermilk off before cooking the plantain stem.

If plantain stem is unavailable, fresh or canned bamboo shoots may be substituted — the texture is similar, but the flavour will be slightly different. In South India, cluster beans are often used instead of plantain stem.

ginger. Sauté for a few seconds. Now add the mashed potato, salt to taste, ground turmeric, and grated coconut. Mix well.

Cook for 1 minute, until thoroughly blended. Remove from the heat. Add the lemon juice.

Garnish the poriyal with chopped coriander leaves. Serve hot.

Sweet potatoes made this way have an unusual hot but sweet taste.

MASHED POTATO PORIYAL

Urulaikizhangu Podimas

PREPARATION TIME: 10 MIN. COOKING TIME: 30 MIN.
SERVES 4

500 g (1 lb) potatoes
2 green chillies (chili peppers), slit sideways
a piece of fresh ginger (2½ cm/1 in long), finely chopped
salt to taste
½ teaspoon ground turmeric
2 tablespoons grated fresh coconut
or 2½ tablespoons flaked coconut
juice of 1 lemon
1 bunch of coriander (Chinese parsley) leaves,
finely chopped

FOR TEMPERING

2 teaspoons oil
1 teaspoon brown mustard seeds
1 teaspoon cumin seeds
1 teaspoon black gram dal (washed urad dal),
picked over and rinsed
1 teaspoon Bengal gram dal (yellow split peas, chana dal),
picked over and rinsed
1 red chilli (chili pepper), halved
½ teaspoon asafoetida powder
a few curry leaves

Method

Boil the potatoes in their jackets. Peel, mash and set aside.

TEMPERING: Heat 2 teaspoons oil in a heavy saucepan. Add the mustard seeds, cumin seeds, black gram dal, Bengal gram dal, red chilli, asafoetida powder, and curry leaves. When the mustard seeds splutter, add the slit green chillies and finely chopped

BEAN DAL PORIYAL

Beans Parupu Usili

PREPARATION TIME: 1 HR 15 MIN. COOKING TIME: 30 MIN.
SERVES 6

1 cup (6 oz) red gram dal (pigeon peas, toor dal),
picked over and rinsed
3 cups (24 fl oz) water
4–5 red chillies (chili peppers)
salt to taste
½ teaspoon asafoetida powder
500 g (1 lb) green or string beans, finely chopped
a little water

FOR TEMPERING

2 tablespoons oil
1 teaspoon brown mustard seeds
1 teaspoon Bengal gram dal (yellow split peas, chana dal),
picked over and rinsed
1 teaspoon black gram dal (washed urad dal),
picked over and rinsed
1 red chilli (chili pepper), halved
½ teaspoon cumin seeds
a few curry leaves

Method

Soak the red gram dal and the red chillies in 3 cups (24 fl oz) water for 1 hour. Drain off water. Place dal and red chillies in an electric blender or food processor. Add salt to taste and asafoetida powder. Blend ingredients to a smooth paste. Set aside.

In a heavy frying pan or skillet, cook the beans until tender, adding salt to taste and only just enough water to prevent the beans from scorching. Set aside.

TEMPERING: In the same pan, heat 2 tablespoons oil. Add mustard seeds, Bengal gram dal, black gram dal, halved red chilli, cumin seeds, and a few curry leaves.

When the mustard seeds splutter, add the red gram dal paste. Sauté over a low heat, stirring occasionally, until the mixture is well cooked and crisp (resembling breadcrumbs, but not hard. Add the cooked beans and sauté for 2–3 minutes, until everything is thoroughly blended. Serve hot.

In South India, cluster beans are often cooked in the same way. For variation, try chopped cabbage, cauliflower or fenugreek leaves instead of green beans. If you are health-conscious, steam the paste, crumble and add to the cooked vegetable instead of sautéing with the spices. Use slightly less oil for tempering in this case.

STUFFED EGGPLANT PORIYAL
Ennai Kathirikkai

PREPARATION TIME: 30 MIN. COOKING TIME: 30 MIN.
SERVES 4

500 g (1 lb) small eggplants (aubergines)

STUFFING

½ coconut, grated (approx. ½–¾ cup flaked coconut)
1 teaspoon oil
1 tablespoon coriander seeds
¾ tablespoon black gram dal (washed urad dal),
picked over and rinsed
¾ tablespoon Bengal gram dal (yellow split peas, chana dal),
picked over and rinsed
1 teaspoon cumin seeds
½ teaspoon asafoetida powder
8 red chillies (chili peppers)
salt to taste
a lemon-sized piece of tamarind pulp
a little water

FOR TEMPERING

3 tablespoons oil
1 teaspoon brown mustard seeds
1 teaspoon cumin seeds
1 teaspoon black gram dal (washed urad dal),
picked over and rinsed
1 teaspoon Bengal gram dal (yellow split peas, chana dal),
picked over and rinsed
1 red chilli (chili pepper), halved
a few curry leaves

Method

STUFFING: Place the grated coconut in a heavy saucepan. Dry-roast until golden brown in colour.

Meanwhile, in a heavy frying pan or skillet, heat 1 teaspoon oil. Add the coriander seeds, black gram dal, Bengal gram dal, cumin seeds, asafoetida powder, red chillies, and salt to taste. Sauté for 2–3 minutes. Place mixture in an electric blender or food processor. Add the roasted coconut and the tamarind pulp. Add just enough water to blend ingredients to a thick paste. Blend or process. Set paste aside.

Slit the eggplants into quarters lengthways, without cutting them through entirely.* Fill the slits with the stuffing and set the eggplants aside.

TEMPERING: Heat 3 tablespoons oil in a heavy frying pan or skillet. Add the mustard seeds, cumin seeds, black gram dal, Bengal gram dal, halved red chilli, and a few curry leaves.

When the mustard seeds splutter, add the stuffed eggplants, salt to taste, and a little water. Sprinkle the leftover stuffing, if any, over the eggplants in the pan. Cover and simmer over a low heat until the eggplants are tender.

Remove the lid and sauté for a few more minutes, without stirring too much. Take care not to break the eggplant.

Serve hot with rice.

* Slit the eggplants into quarters only after the stuffing is ready, otherwise they will become discoloured.

Stuffed Eggplant Poriyal tastes delicious even when only served with plain hot rice.

Try the same stuffing with small sweet peppers (capsicum), if they are in season.

A paste made from 3/4 cup (4 oz) roasted peanuts, 1 teaspoon chilli powder, ½ teaspoon ground turmeric, and salt to taste is equally delicious. Stuff the eggplants as usual and cook until tender. Add 2 medium-sized chopped tomatoes, stir gently for a couple of minutes, and serve.

OPPOSITE – *Stuffed Eggplant Poriyal*
PREVIOUS PAGE – *Bean Dal Poriyal (top left) and Mashed Potato Poriyal (bottom right)*

MASALA BEANS PORIYAL

PREPARATION TIME: 30 MIN. COOKING TIME: 30 MIN.
SERVES 4

500 g (1 lb) green or string beans, finely chopped
salt to taste
a little water

MASALA

2 teaspoons oil
3 tablespoons Bengal gram dal (yellow split peas,
chana dal), picked over and rinsed
1 tablespoon black gram dal (washed urad dal),
picked over and rinsed
2 tablespoons coriander seeds
4 red chillies (chili peppers)
1/2 teaspoon asafoetida powder
4 tablespoons grated fresh coconut
or 5 1/2 tablespoons flaked coconut
a marble-sized piece of tamarind pulp
a little water
salt to taste

FOR TEMPERING

1 tablespoon oil
1 teaspoon brown mustard seeds
1 teaspoon Bengal gram dal (yellow split peas, chana dal),
picked over and rinsed
1 teaspoon black gram dal (washed urad dal),
picked over and rinsed
1 red chilli (chili pepper), halved
1/2 teaspoon asafoetida powder
1 teaspoon cumin seeds
a few curry leaves

Method

MASALA: Heat 2 teaspoons oil in a heavy frying pan or skillet. Add the Bengal gram dal, black gram dal, coriander seeds, red chillies, and asafoetida powder. Sauté for 2–3 minutes. Place mixture in an electric blender or food processor. Add the grated coconut and tamarind pulp. Blend ingredients to a thick paste, adding just enough water to make the paste smooth. Add salt to taste. Set the paste aside.

To a heavy frying pan or skillet, add the finely chopped beans, salt to taste, and a little water (just enough to prevent the beans from scorching). Cook over a low heat until the beans are tender.* Remove from the pan and set aside.

TEMPERING: In the same pan, heat 1 tablespoon oil. Add the mustard seeds, Bengal gram dal, black gram dal, halved red chilli, asafoetida powder, cumin seeds, and a few curry leaves.

When the mustard seeds splutter, add the ground masala paste. Cook over a low heat for 5–7 minutes, until the mixture is dry and crisp.

Now add the cooked beans to the masala. Cook for another 2–3 minutes, until the masala blends well with the beans.

Serve hot with rice.

* Add very little water with the green beans, just enough to cook them. Otherwise, the beans will be overcooked and may become soggy and lose their green colour.

This recipe is often cooked with cluster beans in South India. You may like to try sweet peppers (capsicum) instead of the beans.

Masala Beans Poriyal goes particularly well with Buttermilk Sambar (p. 6) and Mysore Rasam (p. 28). It also tastes delicious when simply mixed with plain cooked rice and perhaps a few drops of hot ghee.

COLOCASIA ROAST

Chepangkizhangu Roast

PREPARATION TIME: 10 MIN. COOKING TIME: 1 HR 30 MIN.
SERVES 4

1 kg (2 lbs) colocasia (arbi)*
1/2 teaspoon ground turmeric
salt to taste
1 tablespoon curry powder (see p. 139)

FOR TEMPERING

2 tablespoons oil
1 teaspoon brown mustard seeds
1 teaspoon cumin seeds
1 teaspoon Bengal gram dal (yellow split peas, chana dal),
picked over and rinsed
1 teaspoon black gram dal (washed urad dal),
picked over and rinsed
1 red chilli (chili pepper), halved
1/2 teaspoon asafoetida powder
a few curry leaves

Method

Boil the colocasia in its jacket until cooked, about 45 minutes. Peel and dice into 1 cm (½ in) cubes. Set aside.

TEMPERING: Heat 2 tablespoons oil in a heavy frying pan or skillet. Add the mustard seeds, cumin seeds, Bengal gram dal, black gram dal, halved red chilli, asafoetida powder, and a few curry leaves.

When the mustard seeds splutter, add the diced colocasia, ground turmeric, and salt to taste. Cook over a low heat for at least 30 minutes, turning the colocasia every 5 minutes. Take extra care not to break the pieces as you do so.

Roast colocasia until golden. Sprinkle with the curry powder. Mix well, but with care.

Serve immediately.

* If fresh colocasia is unavailable, you may be able to buy it canned from Indian markets or Asian food stores.

Make crunchy Potato Roast the same way, using boiled, peeled and diced potatoes.

ABOVE – *Masala Beans Poriyal (top left) and Colocasia Roast (below right)*

PLANTAIN PORIYAL
Vazhakkai Poriyal

PREPARATION TIME: 20 MIN. COOKING TIME: 25 MIN.
SERVES 4

a lemon-sized piece of tamarind pulp
¾ cup (6 fl oz) hot water
3 raw green plantains
½ teaspoon ground turmeric
salt to taste
2 green chillies (chili peppers), slit sideways
1 tablespoon curry powder (see p. 139)
2 tablespoons grated fresh coconut
or 2½ tablespoons flaked coconut

FOR TEMPERING

2 teaspoons oil
1 teaspoon brown mustard seeds
1 teaspoon cumin seeds
1 teaspoon black gram dal (washed urad dal),
picked over and rinsed
1 teaspoon Bengal gram dal (yellow split peas, chana dal),
picked over and rinsed
1 red chilli (chili pepper), halved
¼ teaspoon asafoetida powder
a few curry leaves

Method

Soak the tamarind in ¾ cup (6 fl oz) hot water for 15 minutes. Strain the tamarind water into another container, squeezing as much liquid as possible out of the tamarind pulp. Discard pulp. Set the juice aside.

Peel and chop the green plantain into 1 cm (½ in) pieces. Add the chopped plantain, tamarind juice, ground turmeric, and salt to taste to a heavy saucepan. Cover pan with a lid and cook over a low heat until the plantain is tender and dry. Set aside.

TEMPERING: Heat 2 teaspoons oil in a heavy saucepan. Add the mustard seeds, cumin seeds, black gram dal, Bengal gram dal, halved red chilli, asafoetida powder, and a few curry leaves.

When the mustard seeds splutter, add the slit green chillies, cooked plantain, curry powder and coconut. Cook for 1 minute, until thoroughly blended.

Serve hot with rice.

OPPOSITE PAGE – *Plantain Poriyal (top left) and Potato Masala (bottom right)*

POTATO MASALA
Potato Paliya

PREPARATION TIME: 30 MIN. COOKING TIME: 50 MIN.
SERVES 4

500 g (1 lb) potatoes
2–3 green chillies (chili peppers), finely chopped
a piece of fresh ginger (2½ cm/1 in long),
scraped and finely chopped
2 medium-sized onions, finely chopped
2 tomatoes, finely chopped (optional)
salt to taste
½ teaspoon ground turmeric
1 cup (8 fl oz) water
½ cup (3 oz) boiled green peas (optional)
1 small bunch of coriander (Chinese parsley) leaves,
finely chopped (to garnish)

FOR TEMPERING

1 tablespoon oil
1 teaspoon brown mustard seeds
1 teaspoon cumin seeds
1 teaspoon black gram dal (washed urad dal),
picked over and rinsed
1 teaspoon Bengal gram dal (yellow split peas, chana dal),
picked over and rinsed
1 red chilli (chili pepper), halved
½ teaspoon asafoetida powder
a few curry leaves

Method

Boil the potatoes in their jackets until cooked. Peel, mash and set aside.

TEMPERING: Heat 1 tablespoon oil in a heavy saucepan. Add the mustard seeds, cumin seeds, black gram dal, Bengal gram dal, halved red chilli, asafoetida powder, and a few curry leaves.

When the mustard seeds splutter, add the finely chopped green chillies, ginger, onion and tomatoes (if used). Sauté for 2–3 minutes.

Add the salt to taste, ground turmeric, and 1 cup (8 fl oz) water. Cover pan with a lid. Simmer for about 5 minutes, until the onions are well cooked. Add the mashed potatoes and boiled peas (if used). Cook for another 2 minutes, until thoroughly blended.

Garnish with finely chopped coriander leaves. Serve hot with Masala Dosai (p. 87) or puris.

DAL KOOTU
Poritha Kootu

PREPARATION TIME: 25 MIN. COOKING TIME: 2 HRS
SERVES 4

1/4 cup or 4 tablespoons green gram dal (split mung beans,
moong dal), picked over and rinsed
1 cup (8 fl oz) water
1/2 cup (3 oz) green or string beans, finely chopped
1 carrot, finely chopped
1 potato, diced
1/2 cup (3 oz) shelled green peas
salt to taste
1/2 teaspoon ground turmeric
curry leaves (to garnish)

PASTE

1 teaspoon oil
3/4 teaspoon cumin seeds
1 teaspoon black peppercorns
2 red chillies (chili peppers)
1/2 teaspoon asafoetida powder
2 tablespoons grated fresh coconut or
2 1/2 tablespoons flaked coconut
a little water

FOR TEMPERING

2 teaspoons ghee
1 teaspoon brown mustard seeds
1/2 teaspoon cumin seeds
1 teaspoon black gram dal (washed urad dal),
picked over and rinsed
1 red chilli (chili pepper), halved
a few curry leaves

Method

Rinse green gram dal well. Place in a heavy saucepan. Add 1 cup
(8 fl oz) water and bring to the boil. When boiling, cover
pan, leaving lid slightly ajar. Lower heat, and simmer gently for
1 1/2 hours. Stir several times during the last 30 minutes. Set aside
without draining.

PASTE: Heat the oil in a heavy frying pan or skillet. Add cumin
seeds, black peppercorns, red chillies, and asafoetida powder.
Sauté for 2–3 minutes. Place in an electric blender or food
processor. Add the coconut and very little water. Blend to a fine
paste. Set aside.

In a heavy saucepan, bring the beans, carrot, potato, green peas,
salt to taste, and ground turmeric to the boil. Add the undrained
cooked dal. Simmer for 2–3 minutes. Now add the paste. Simmer
until thoroughly blended.

TEMPERING: Heat the ghee in a heavy frying pan or skillet. Add
the mustard seeds, cumin seeds, black gram dal, halved red chilli,
and a few curry leaves. When the mustard seeds splutter, add to
the kootu.

Garnish with extra curry leaves to serve.

*For an alternative paste, use 1 teaspoon cumin seeds, 1 teaspoon black
peppercorns, 2 green chillies, and 3 tablespoons grated fresh coconut
(4 tablespoons flaked). This is delicious with spinach or snake gourd.*

TAMARIND KOOTU
Pulippu Kootu

PREPARATION TIME: 30 MIN. COOKING TIME: 1 HR 30 MIN.
SERVES 4

4 tablespoons red gram dal (pigeon peas, toor dal),
picked over and rinsed
4 tablespoons Bengal gram dal (yellow split peas,
chana dal), picked over and rinsed
2 cups (16 fl oz) water
a marble-sized piece of tamarind pulp
1 cup (8 fl oz) hot water
500 g (1 lb) ash gourd, peeled and finely chopped
salt to taste
1/2 teaspoon ground turmeric

PASTE

2 teaspoons oil
1 1/2 teaspoons black peppercorns
2 teaspoons black gram dal (washed urad dal),
picked over and rinsed
1 tablespoon Bengal gram dal (yellow split peas,
chana dal), picked over and rinsed
1/2 teaspoon asafoetida powder
1 tablespoon coriander seeds
1 red chilli (chili pepper)
4 tablespoons grated fresh coconut or
5 1/2 tablespoons flaked coconut
a little water

FOR TEMPERING

3 teaspoons ghee
1 teaspoon brown mustard seeds
1 teaspoon black gram dal (washed urad dal),
picked over and rinsed
2 tablespoons raw peanuts
1 red chilli (chili pepper), halved
a few curry leaves

Method

Rinse both red gram dal and Bengal gram dal well. Place in a heavy saucepan. Cover with 2 cups (16 fl oz) water and bring to the boil. When boiling, cover pan, leaving lid slightly ajar. Lower the heat, and simmer dal gently for 1½ hours. Stir several times during the last 30 minutes of cooking. Set aside without draining.

Soak the tamarind in 1 cup (8 fl oz) hot water for 15 minutes. Strain the tamarind water into another container, squeezing as much liquid as possible out of the tamarind pulp. Discard pulp. Set the juice aside.

PASTE: Heat the oil in a heavy frying pan or skillet. Add black peppercorns, black gram dal, Bengal gram dal, asafoetida powder, coriander seeds, and red chilli. Sauté for 2–3 minutes. Place in an electric blender or food processor. Add the grated coconut and a little water. Blend ingredients to a fine paste. Set aside.

TEMPERING: Heat the ghee in a heavy saucepan. Add the mustard seeds, black gram dal, raw peanuts, halved red chilli, and a few curry leaves.

When the mustard seeds splutter and the peanuts are sautéed, add the finely chopped ash gourd, salt to taste, ground turmeric, and tamarind juice. Simmer until the gourd is tender. Now add the undrained cooked dals. Simmer until thoroughly blended. Add the paste and cook for a few more minutes.

Serve hot with rice.

Make this kootu with any vegetable other than okra (lady's fingers), bitter gourd (bitter melon) or colocasia as they have a high water content and tend to become mushy when cooked with other vegetables.

ABOVE – *Tamarind Kootu (top left) and Dal Kootu (bottom right)*

BUTTERMILK KOOTU
Moru Kootu

PREPARATION TIME: 25 MIN. COOKING TIME: 20 MIN.
SERVES 4

2 medium-sized raw green plantains,
skinned and finely chopped*
2 small eggplants (aubergines), finely chopped
1 ckoko (chayote), peeled and finely chopped or
100 g (3–4 oz) snake gourd
1 ripe tomato, quartered
salt to taste
½ teaspoon ground turmeric
water to cover

PASTE

2 teaspoons oil
3 red chillies (chili peppers)
2 teaspoons coriander seeds
1 teaspoon Bengal gram dal (yellow split peas,
chana dal), picked over and rinsed
½ teaspoon fenugreek seeds
½ coconut, grated (approx. ½–¾ cup flaked coconut)
2 green chillies (chili peppers)
a little water
1 cup (8 fl oz) plain yogurt (see p. 136)

FOR TEMPERING

2 teaspoons ghee
1 teaspoon brown mustard seeds
a few curry leaves

Method

PASTE: Heat 2 teaspoons oil in a heavy frying pan or skillet. Add red chillies, coriander seeds, Bengal gram dal, and fenugreek seeds. Sauté for 2–3 minutes. Place in an electric blender or food processor. Add the grated coconut, green chillies, and a little water. Blend to a fine paste. Add the yogurt and mix well. Set aside.

TEMPERING: Heat 2 teaspoons ghee in a heavy saucepan. Add mustard seeds and a few curry leaves.

When the mustard seeds splutter, add the finely chopped plantain, eggplant, choko, snake gourd and quartered tomato. Add the salt to taste, ground turmeric, and sufficient water to just cover the vegetables. Cover pan and cook vegetables over a low heat until tender.

Now add the paste. Heat the kootu through gently, so the yogurt does not curdle. Serve hot with rice.

* If plantain is unavailable, use 250 g (8 oz) yam. This kootu can also be made with any squash vegetable of your choice: bottle gourd, pumpkin, ash gourd, etc.

EGGPLANT RASAVANGY
Kathirikkai Rasavangy

PREPARATION TIME: 20 MIN. COOKING TIME: 1 HR 50 MIN.
SERVES 4

½ cup (3 oz) red gram dal (pigeon peas, toor dal),
picked over and rinsed
2 cups (16 fl oz) water
a marble-sized piece of tamarind pulp
1 cup (8 fl oz) hot water
2 green chillies (chili peppers), slit sideways
1 small tomato, chopped
155 g (5 oz) ripe eggplants (aubergines),
quartered lengthways
½ teaspoon ground turmeric
½ teaspoon sambar powder (see Sambar Powder 1, p. 136)
1 tablespoon powdered jaggery
salt to taste
coriander (Chinese parsley) leaves, chopped (to garnish)

PASTE

1 teaspoon oil
1½ tablespoons coriander seeds
2 red chillies (chili peppers)
½ teaspoon asafoetida powder
4 tablespoons grated fresh coconut or
5½ tablespoons flaked coconut
a little water

FOR TEMPERING

2 teaspoons ghee
1 teaspoon brown mustard seeds
1 red chilli (chili pepper), halved
a few curry leaves

OPPOSITE – *Eggplant Rasavangy (top left) and*
Buttermilk Kootu (bottom right)

Method

Wash the red gram dal well. Drain. Place dal in a heavy saucepan. Cover with 2 cups (16 fl oz) water and bring to the boil. When boiling, cover pan with a lid, leaving slightly ajar. Lower the heat, and simmer dal gently for 1½ hours. Stir several times during the last 30 minutes of cooking. Set dal aside without draining.

Soak the tamarind in 1 cup (8 fl oz) hot water for 15 minutes. Strain the tamarind water into another container, squeezing as much liquid as possible out of the tamarind pulp. Discard pulp. Set the juice aside.

PASTE: Heat 1 teaspoon oil in a heavy frying pan or skillet. Add coriander seeds, red chillies, and asafoetida powder. Sauté for 2–3 minutes. Place in an electric blender or food processor. Add the grated coconut and a very little water. Blend to a fine paste. Set aside.

TEMPERING: Heat 2 teaspoons ghee in a heavy saucepan. Add the mustard seeds, halved red chilli, and a few curry leaves.

When the mustard seeds splutter, add the slit green chillies, chopped tomato, and quartered eggplants. Now add ground turmeric, sambar powder, tamarind juice, jaggery, and salt to taste. Cook over a low heat until the vegetables are done. Add the undrained cooked dal and paste. Simmer for a couple of minutes, until thoroughly blended.

Garnish with chopped coriander leaves. Serve hot with rice.

Choko (chayote) and kohlrabi also make tasty rasavangies.

MIXED VEGETABLE KOOTU
Avial

PREPARATION TIME: 30 MIN. COOKING TIME: 30 MIN.
SERVES 4

155 g (5 oz) yam
155 g (5 oz) ash gourd
2 raw green plantains
2 drumsticks*
1 potato
1/2 cup (3 oz) shelled green peas
salt to taste
1/2 teaspoon ground turmeric
1/4 cup (2 fl oz) coconut oil
a few curry leaves

PASTE

1/2 coconut, grated (approx. 1/2–3/4 cup flaked coconut)
6–7 green chillies (chili peppers)
1 teaspoon cumin seeds
a little water
1 cup (8 fl oz) plain yogurt (see p. 136)

Method

PASTE: Place the grated coconut, green chillies, and cumin seeds in an electric blender or food processor. Blend ingredients to a fine paste, adding very little water. Mix the yogurt through the paste. Set aside.

Peel and chop the yam, ash gourd, plantain, drumstick, and potato into 8 cm (3 in) lengths. Cook each vegetable separately, including the shelled peas, in a heavy saucepan. Add very little water to the pan each time, just enough to prevent scorching.

Place all the cooked vegetables back in the saucepan together. Add salt to taste and ground turmeric. Now add the paste. Heat through gently, so yogurt does not curdle.

Lastly, add coconut oil and a few curry leaves. Mix thoroughly and remove from the heat immediately.

Serve hot with rice.

If drumsticks are unavailable, either fresh or canned, you can omit this ingredient entirely. As 'Avial' means medley, you can make a medley of any vegetables of your choice — carrots, green or string beans, potatoes, fresh green peas, zucchini (courgettes) — it's up to you.

Carrots, beans and cluster beans are common additions in South India. However, never use vegetables such as colocasia and okra (lady's fingers), which have a high water content. They tend to become mushy when cooked with other vegetables.

COCONUT YAM KOOTU
Erisherri

PREPARATION TIME: 20 MIN. COOKING TIME: 20 MIN.
SERVES 6

1/2 coconut, grated (approx. 1/2–3/4
cup flaked coconut)
2 tablespoons coconut oil
500 g (1 lb) yams
3 green plantains*
2 teaspoons chilli powder
1 teaspoon ground black pepper
1/2 teaspoon ground turmeric
salt to taste
1 teaspoon cumin seeds

FOR TEMPERING

1 tablespoon coconut oil
1 teaspoon brown mustard seeds
1 red chilli (chili pepper), halved
a few curry leaves

Method

Sauté the grated coconut in the 2 tablespoons coconut oil until golden brown. Set aside.

Peel both the yams and plantains. Chop into 1 cm (1/2 in) pieces. Place in a heavy saucepan and add sufficient water to just cover the vegetables.

Now add the chilli powder, ground black pepper, ground turmeric, and salt to taste. Cover saucepan with a lid and simmer over a low heat until the vegetables are tender.

In the meantime, take half the sautéed coconut and place in an electric blender or food processor. Add the cumin seeds and blend ingredients into a paste.

Now add this paste to the cooked vegetables and simmer for 2–3 minutes more. Mash the vegetables and set aside still in the saucepan.

TEMPERING: Heat 1 tablespoon coconut oil in a heavy frying pan or skillet. Add the mustard seeds, halved red chilli and a few curry leaves.

When the mustard seeds splutter, add this mixture to the mashed vegetables. Heat kootu through gently.

Just before turning off the heat, add the remaining sautéed coconut.

Serve hot with rice and poppadoms.

Coconut Yam Kootu originally comes from the state of Kerala. This dish is often made with tapioca instead of green plantains. If plantains are unavailable, use 1½ cups (5 oz) tapioca instead.

ABOVE – *Snake Gourd Kootu (top left) and Mashed Amaranth (bottom right)*
PREVIOUS PAGE – *Mixed Vegetable Kootu (top left) and Coconut Yam Kootu (bottom right)*

SNAKE GOURD KOOTU
Pudalangai Milagu Kootal

PREPARATION TIME: 20 MIN. COOKING TIME: 1 HR 35 MIN.
SERVES 4

½ cup (3 oz) red gram dal (pigeon peas, toor dal)
2 cups (16 fl oz) water
1 medium-sized snake gourd (500 g/1 lb), finely chopped
2 cups (16 fl oz) water (extra)
½ teaspoon ground turmeric
salt to taste

PASTE

2 teaspoons coconut oil
2–3 tablespoons black gram dal (washed urad dal),
picked over and rinsed
3–4 red chillies (chili peppers)
½ coconut, grated (approx. ½ cup flaked coconut)
3–4 teaspoons cumin seeds
1 teaspoon uncooked rice
a little water

FOR TEMPERING

2 teaspoons coconut oil
1 teaspoon brown mustard seeds
1 red chilli (chili pepper), halved
a few curry leaves

Method

Wash the red gram dal well. Drain. Place dal in a heavy saucepan. Cover with 2 cups (16 fl oz) water and bring to the boil. When boiling, cover pan with a lid, leaving slightly ajar. Lower the heat, and simmer dal gently for 1½ hours. Stir several times during the last 30 minutes of cooking. Set dal aside without draining.

PASTE: Heat 2 teaspoons coconut oil in a heavy frying pan or skillet. Add the black gram dal and 3–4 red chillies. Sauté for 2–3 minutes. Place mixture in an electric blender or food processor. Add the grated coconut, cumin seeds, uncooked rice, and just a little water. Blend ingredients to a fine paste. Set aside.

Place finely chopped snake gourd in a heavy saucepan. Add 2 cups (16 fl oz) water, ground turmeric, and salt to taste. When the gourd is tender, add the undrained cooked dal. Simmer until thoroughly blended.

Add the paste to the kootu and cook for a few more minutes. Remove from the heat.

TEMPERING: Heat 2 teaspoons coconut oil in a heavy frying pan or skillet. Add the mustard seeds, halved red chilli, and a few curry leaves. When the mustard seeds splutter, add this mixture to the kootu.

Serve hot with rice.

For an interesting variation, use cabbage, kohlrabi, amaranth leaves, or spinach leaves instead of snake gourd.

MASHED AMARANTH
Keerai Masial

PREPARATION TIME: 30 MIN. COOKING TIME: 1 HR 40 MIN.
SERVES 4

¼ cup or 4 tablespoons green gram dal (split mung beans,
moong dal), picked over and rinsed
1 cup (8 fl oz water)
2 bunches of amaranth leaves*
salt to taste

FOR TEMPERING

2 teaspoons ghee
1 teaspoon brown mustard seeds
1 teaspoon cumin seeds
1 teaspoon black gram dal (washed urad dal), picked over and rinsed
1 red chilli (chili pepper), halved
½ teaspoon asafoetida powder

Method

Rinse green gram dal well. Place in a heavy saucepan. Add 1 cup (8 fl oz) water and bring to the boil. When boiling, cover pan, leaving lid slightly ajar. Lower heat, and simmer gently for 1½ hours. Stir several times during the last 30 minutes. Set aside without draining.

Wash the amaranth leaves and chop finely. Lightly boil or steam, taking care the leaves do not lose their colour. Blend or process to a purée. Set aside. Add salt to taste to the undrained cooked dal. Mix well and reheat.

TEMPERING: Heat 2 teaspoons ghee in a heavy frying pan or skillet. Add the mustard seeds, cumin seeds, black gram dal, halved red chilli, and asafoetida powder.

When the mustard seeds splutter, add this mixture to the mashed amaranth. Mix with the cooked dal and heat through gently.

Serve hot with rice.

* Fresh spinach leaves may be used instead of amaranth leaves.

POTATO SONG

PREPARATION TIME: 10 MIN. COOKING TIME: 45 MIN.
SERVES 4

500 g (1 lb) large potatoes
a lemon-sized piece of tamarind pulp
1 cup (8 fl oz) hot water
4 large onions, finely chopped
salt to taste
3 teaspoons chilli powder
a lemon-sized piece of jaggery
1½ teaspoons ground coriander
1 bunch of coriander (Chinese parsley) leaves,
finely chopped (to garnish)

FOR TEMPERING

3 tablespoons coconut oil
1 teaspoon brown mustard seeds
a few curry leaves

Method

Boil the potatoes in their jackets until cooked. Take care not to overcook as they will crumble when diced. Peel and cut into 1 cm (½ in) cubes. Set aside.

Soak the tamarind in 1 cup (8 fl oz) hot water for 15 minutes. Strain the tamarind water into another container, squeezing as much liquid as possible out of the tamarind pulp. Discard pulp. Set the juice aside.

TEMPERING:
Heat 3 tablespoons coconut oil in a heavy saucepan. Add the mustard seeds and a few curry leaves.

When the mustard seeds splutter, add the finely chopped onions. Sauté until the onions are golden brown in colour.

Add the diced potatoes and sauté for 2–3 minutes longer.

Now add the tamarind juice, salt to taste, chilli powder, and jaggery. Simmer for a couple of minutes.

Lastly, add the ground coriander and simmer again, until thoroughly blended. Remove from the heat.

Garnish with the chopped coriander leaves. Serve hot with puris or chapattis.

Make this dish a day earlier than needed. The potatoes soak up the tart tamarind gravy and become mouth-wateringly crumbly.

OPPOSITE – *Potato Song (bottom left) and Vegetable Korma (top right)*

VEGETABLE KORMA

PREPARATION TIME: 20 MIN. COOKING TIME: 35 MIN.
SERVES 4

1 cup (approx. 6 oz) finely chopped green or string beans
1 cup (approx. 6 oz) finely chopped carrots
2 potatoes, finely chopped
½ cup (3 oz) shelled green peas
1 large tomato, chopped
salt to taste
1 tablespoon ghee
a few bay leaves
½ bunch of coriander (Chinese parsley) leaves (to garnish)

PASTE

½ coconut, grated (approx. ½ cup flaked coconut)
6–8 green chillies (chili peppers)
1 small onion, chopped
a piece of fresh ginger (1 cm/½ in long)
½ teaspoon ground turmeric
1 small bunch of coriander (Chinese parsley) leaves
a little water

MASALA

1 tablespoon aniseed
a small piece of cinnamon bark
6 cloves
2 cardamom pods
1 tablespoon poppy seeds

Method

PASTE: Place the grated coconut, green chillies, chopped onion, ginger, ground turmeric and coriander leaves in an electric blender or food processor, adding only a little water. Blend ingredients to a fine paste. Set aside.

MASALA: Place the aniseed, cinnamon bark, cloves, cardamom pods, and poppy seeds in a heavy saucepan. Dry-roast spices until they give off a strong aroma. Grind to a fine powder in an electric blender or food processor. Set aside.

Place the finely chopped green beans, carrots, and potatoes in a heavy saucepan. Add sufficient water to just cover the vegetables. Cover pan with a lid, and cook until the vegetables are tender. Now add the green peas, chopped tomato and salt to taste. Simmer for 1–2 minutes.

Add the paste. Stir thoroughly before sprinkling in the masala powder. Stir the korma thoroughly once more.

Heat 1 tablespoon ghee in a heavy frying pan or skillet. Sauté the bay leaves for 2–3 minutes, then add to the korma.

Garnish with coriander leaves. Serve hot with phulkas, puris or parathas.

This dish is also an excellent accompaniment to idlis and dosais (see 'Snacks', pp. 83–107).

MIXED VEGETABLE SAGU
Sagu

PREPARATION TIME: 30 MIN. COOKING TIME: 30 MIN.
SERVES 4

approx. 1 cup chopped mixed vegetables (e.g. choko [chayote], cabbage and green or string beans)
2 carrots
1 potato
1 onion, finely chopped
250 g (8 oz) shelled green peas
salt to taste
½ teaspoon ground turmeric
a little water
a little oil
2 tablespoons raw cashew nuts (for garnish)
1 bunch of coriander (Chinese parsley) leaves (to garnish)

PASTE

4–5 green chillies (chili peppers)
1 tablespoon fried gram dal*
¼ teaspoon black peppercorns
3 teaspoons ground coriander
1 teaspoon cumin seeds
1 small stick cinnamon bark
2–3 cloves
4–5 tablespoons grated fresh coconut or
5½–6½ tablespoons flaked coconut
a little water

FOR TEMPERING

2 tablespoons ghee
1 teaspoon brown mustard seeds
1 red chilli (chili pepper), halved

1 teaspoon black gram dal (washed urad dal), picked over and rinsed
½ teaspoon asafoetida powder
a few curry leaves

Method

Peel and prepare mixed vegetables, carrots and potato as necessary. Chop or dice into 1 cm (½ in) pieces.

PASTE: Place green chillies, fried gram dal, black peppercorns, ground coriander, cumin seeds, cinnamon stick, cloves, and grated coconut in an electric blender or food processor. Add only very little water and blend ingredients to a paste. Set aside.

TEMPERING: Heat 2 tablespoons ghee in a heavy saucepan. Add the mustard seeds, halved red chilli, black gram dal, asafoetida powder, and a few curry leaves.

When the mustard seeds splutter, add the finely chopped onion and sauté for 2–3 minutes.

Now add the chopped mixed vegetables, peas, salt to taste, ground turmeric, and just enough water to cover the vegetables. Simmer until the vegetables are tender.

Meanwhile, add a little oil to a pan and gently sauté the cashew nuts. Set aside.

Add the ground paste to the sagu and simmer for a few minutes more.

Garnish the sagu with the chopped coriander leaves and sautéed cashew nuts. Serve hot with puris or parathas.

* Fried gram dal is roasted and puffed Bengal gram dal (yellow split peas, chana dal). It should be available in Indian markets or Asian food stores. If unavailable, dry-roast 1 tablespoon Bengal gram dal in a heavy frying pan or skillet for 2–3 minutes and use as a substitute.

OPPOSITE – *Mixed Vegetable Sagu*

SALADS

Fresh and crisp, and made with many different types of vegetables, salads may be served with any savoury course of a typical South Indian meal.

Most vegetables are chopped raw, and seasoned lightly or mixed with yogurt. Others are boiled or sautéed just long enough to remove the raw taste, but without losing their crisp and crunchy texture.

Highly nutritious, salads are terrific coolers. Neither a vegetable dish nor a relish, they nevertheless lend variety and zest to any meal.

FRESH CUCUMBER SALAD
Vellarikkai Kosumalli

PREPARATION TIME: 1 HR; COOKING TIME: 3 MIN.
SERVES 4

2 tablespoons green gram dal (split mung beans,
moong dal), picked over and rinsed
1 cup (8 fl oz) water
1 large cucumber, peeled and finely chopped
2–3 tablespoons grated fresh coconut or
2½–4 tablespoons flaked coconut
1 green chilli (chilli pepper), finely chopped
1 small bunch of coriander (Chinese parsley) leaves,
finely chopped
salt to taste
1 tablespoon lemon juice

FOR TEMPERING

2 teaspoons oil
1 teaspoon brown mustard seeds
1 teaspoon cumin seeds
1 teaspoon black gram dal (washed urad dal),
picked over and rinsed
1 teaspoon Bengal gram dal (yellow split peas, chana dal),
picked over and rinsed
½ teaspoon asafoetida powder
1 red chilli (chili pepper), halved
a few curry leaves

Method

Wash the green gram dal well. Soak in 1 cup (8 fl oz) water for
1 hour.

In a bowl, mix the finely chopped cucumber, grated coconut,
green chilli, coriander leaves, salt to taste, and lemon juice. Add
the soaked green gram dal and mix thoroughly.

TEMPERING: Heat 2 teaspoons oil in a heavy frying pan or
skillet. Add the mustard seeds, cumin seeds, black gram dal,
Bengal gram dal, asafoetida powder, halved red chilli, and a few
curry leaves.

When the mustard seeds splutter, add to the salad. Mix
thoroughly.

Serve chilled or at room temperature.

VEGETABLE MEDLEY
Thakkali-Vellarikkai-Carrot
Kosumalli

PREPARATION TIME: 15 MIN. COOKING TIME: 3 MIN.
SERVES 4

1 carrot, peeled and finely chopped
1 cucumber, peeled and finely chopped
1 tomato, finely chopped
1 green chilli (chili pepper), finely chopped
1 small bunch of coriander (Chinese parsley) leaves,
finely chopped
salt to taste
2 tablespoons lemon juice

FOR TEMPERING

2 teaspoons oil
1 teaspoon brown mustard seeds
1 teaspoon cumin seeds
1 teaspoon black gram dal (washed urad dal),
picked over and rinsed
1 red chilli (chili pepper), halved
½ teaspoon asafoetida powder
a few curry leaves

Method

Peel and prepare the vegetables as necessary, including the
tomato, green chilli, and coriander. Place the finely chopped
carrot, cucumber, tomato, green chilli, and coriander in a bowl.
Add the salt to taste, and mix thoroughly. Set aside.

TEMPERING: Heat 2 teaspoons oil, in a heavy frying pan or
skillet. Add the mustard seeds, cumin seeds, black gram dal,
halved red chilli, asafoetida powder, and a few curry leaves.

When the mustard seeds splutter, add this mixture to the
vegetables. Now add the lemon juice, and mix thoroughly.

Serve cold or at room temperature.

*Make your own exciting medley of vegetables: mix and match with
whatever vegetables you choose. Alternatively, make a salad
consisting only of your favourite vegetable.*

OPPOSITE – *Fresh Cucumber Salad (top left) and
Vegetable Medley (bottom right)*

MIXED VEGETABLE CURD SALAD

Vellarikkai-Thakkali-Vengaya Pachadi

PREPARATION TIME: 15 MIN. COOKING TIME: 3 MIN.
SERVES 4

1 medium-sized cucumber, peeled and finely chopped
1 ripe tomato, finely chopped
1 medium-sized onion, finely chopped
1–2 green chillies (chili peppers), finely chopped
1 small bunch of coriander (Chinese parsley) leaves,
finely chopped
2 cups (16 fl oz) fresh plain yogurt (see p. 136)
salt to taste
extra coriander (Chinese parsley) leaves, chopped
(to garnish)

FOR TEMPERING
2 teaspoons oil
1 teaspoon brown mustard seeds
1 teaspoon cumin seeds
1 teaspoon black gram dal (washed urad dal),
picked over and rinsed
1 teaspoon Bengal gram dal (yellow split peas,
chana dal), picked over and rinsed
1/2 teaspoon asafoetida powder
1 red chilli (chili pepper), halved
a few curry leaves

Method

Peel and prepare the vegetables as necessary, including green chillies and coriander. In a bowl, mix the finely chopped cucumber, tomato, onions, green chillies, and coriander leaves with the yogurt, and salt to taste.

TEMPERING: Heat 2 teaspoons oil in a heavy frying pan or skillet. Add the mustard seeds, cumin seeds, black gram dal, Bengal gram dal, asafoetida powder, halved red chilli, and a few curry leaves.

When the mustard seeds splutter, add this mixture to the salad. Mix thoroughly. Garnish with extra chopped coriander leaves.

Serve cold or at room temperature.

For a more distinct flavour rather than a blend of flavours, make this salad with just one of the vegetables you are particularly fond of.

COCONUT CURD SALAD

Thengai Thair Pachadi

PREPARATION TIME: 10 MIN. COOKING TIME: 10 MIN.
SERVES 4

3 tablespoons grated fresh coconut or 4 tablespoons
flaked coconut
4 green chillies (chili peppers)
a piece of fresh ginger (1 cm/1/2 in), finely chopped
1 bunch of coriander (Chinese parsley) leaves, finely chopped
1 cup (8 fl oz) fresh plain yogurt (see p. 136)
salt to taste

FOR TEMPERING
1 1/2 teaspoons oil
1 teaspoon brown mustard seeds
1 teaspoon Bengal gram dal (yellow split peas,
chana dal), picked over and rinsed
1/2 teaspoon black gram dal (washed urad dal),
picked over and rinsed
1/4 teaspoon cumin seeds
1 red chilli (chili pepper), halved
1/4 teaspoon asafoetida powder
a few curry leaves

Method

Place the grated coconut, green chillies, finely chopped ginger, and some of the coriander leaves in an electric blender or food processor. Blend ingredients to a fine paste. Add to the yogurt and mix thoroughly. Add salt to taste. Set aside.

TEMPERING: Heat 1 1/2 teaspoons oil in a heavy frying pan or skillet. Add the mustard seeds, Bengal gram dal, black gram dal, cumin seeds, halved red chilli, asafoetida powder, and a few curry leaves.

When the mustard seeds splutter and the dals turn golden, add this mixture to the salad.

Garnish the salad with the rest of the chopped coriander leaves. Serve cold or at room temperature.

Gooseberry Salad is equally tasty. To make this delicious alternative, simply omit grated coconut and substitute with approx. 1 cup (6 oz) deseeded cape gooseberries (small variety).

OPPOSITE – *Mixed Vegetable Curd Salad (top left) and Coconut Curd Salad (bottom right)*

MANGO CURD SALAD
Mangai Pachadi

PREPARATION TIME: 20 MIN. COOKING TIME: 3 MIN.
SERVES 4

1 small green mango, skinned and finely chopped
2 tablespoons grated fresh coconut or 2½ tablespoons
flaked coconut
4 green chillies (chili peppers)
1 teaspoon cumin seeds
a little water
2 cups (16 fl oz) plain yogurt (see p. 136)
salt to taste
1 bunch of coriander (Chinese parsley) leaves (to garnish)

FOR TEMPERING

1 teaspoon oil
1 teaspoon brown mustard seeds
1 teaspoon cumin seeds
¼ teaspoon asafoetida powder
1 red chilli (chili pepper), halved
a few curry leaves

Method

Place the finely chopped mango, grated coconut, green chillies, and cumin seeds in an electric blender or food processor. Add only a little water and blend ingredients to a fine paste.

In a serving dish, mix the yogurt with the ground paste. Add salt to taste. Set aside.

TEMPERING: Heat 1 teaspoon oil in a heavy frying pan or skillet. Add the mustard seeds, cumin seeds, asafoetida powder, halved red chilli, and a few curry leaves. When the mustard seeds splutter, add this mixture to the salad.

Garnish the salad with coriander leaves. Serve cold or at room temperature.

OPPOSITE – *Mango Curd Salad (top left) and Okra Curd Salad (bottom right)*

OKRA CURD SALAD
Vendakkai Thair Pachadi

PREPARATION TIME: 15 MIN. COOKING TIME: 10 MIN.
SERVES 4

250 g (8 oz) okra (lady's fingers)
salt to taste
1½ cups (12 fl oz) plain yogurt (see p. 136)

FOR TEMPERING

2 teaspoons oil
1 teaspoon brown mustard seeds
1 teaspoon cumin seeds
1 teaspoon black gram dal (washed urad dal),
picked over and rinsed
1 teaspoon Bengal gram dal (yellow split peas,
chana dal), picked over and rinsed
1 red chilli (chili pepper), halved
¼ teaspoon asafoetida powder
a few curry leaves

Method

Stem and finely chop the okra. Set aside.

TEMPERING: Heat 2 teaspoons oil in a heavy frying pan or skillet. Add the mustard seeds, cumin seeds, black gram dal, Bengal gram dal, halved red chilli, asafoetida powder, and a few curry leaves.

When the mustard seeds splutter, add the finely chopped okra. Cook on a low heat until the vegetable is tender.

Add salt to taste, and cook for 1 minute. Allow the okra to cool. Add the well-mixed yogurt and blend thoroughly.

Serve cold or at room temperature.

If you would like to serve the okra as a poriyal rather than a salad, do not add the yogurt.

Always add the salt at the end of cooking the okra. This helps to prevent it from becoming soggy, as okra has a high water content and salt will draw this moisture out.

You can use snake gourd, bottle gourd, white pumpkin or ash gourd, tomato, or sweet pepper (capsicum) instead of okra. If you are using potatoes, boil and dice them, and then use the same seasoning as above.

RICE
DISHES
& POWDERS

You can serve a rice dish with any meal at any time of the day. The rich, heavy rices — such as Spicy Sambar Rice and Tamarind Rice — are a meal in themselves. However, the lighter rice dishes can be served with any course. Take them on picnics and outings, or when travelling. Non-messy, easy to pack and simple to make, rice dishes make tasty and nutritious packed lunches.

~

At any given time, the kitchen shelves of any South Indian home have at least two or three instant powders called 'podis'. Made from a variety of beans or pulses, plus seasonings, podis can be used to make an instant meal especially on days when you are tired or rushed for time.

~

Just mix with rice and ghee, then roast a poppadom … and your food is ready! Round off your meal with a helping of yogurt, and you will satisfy your appetite both quickly and deliciously.

COCONUT RICE
Thengai Sadam

PREPARATION TIME: 10 MIN. COOKING TIME: 30 MIN.
SERVES 4

1 cup (5 oz) long-grained rice
2 tablespoons white sesame seeds (optional)
3 tablespoons ghee
3 tablespoons raw cashew nuts, halved (to garnish)
1/2 coconut, grated (approx. 3/4 cup flaked coconut)
2 green chillies (chili peppers), finely chopped
salt to taste

FOR TEMPERING

2 teaspoons oil
1 teaspoon brown mustard seeds
1 teaspoon cumin seeds
1 teaspoon black gram dal (washed urad dal),
picked over and rinsed
1 teaspoon Bengal gram dal (yellow split peas,
chana dal), picked over and rinsed
1 red chilli (chili pepper), halved
1/2 teaspoon asafoetida powder
a few curry leaves

Method

Cook the rice and set aside.

Dry-roast the sesame seeds (if used) for 2–3 minutes in a heavy saucepan. Blend or process into a fine powder. Set aside.

Heat 2 tablespoons ghee in a heavy frying pan or skillet. Sauté the cashew nuts until golden. Set aside.

In the same pan, heat the remaining 1 tablespoon ghee, and sauté the grated coconut until reddish brown in colour. Set aside.

TEMPERING: Heat 2 teaspoons oil in the pan, and add the mustard seeds, cumin seeds, black gram dal, Bengal gram dal, halved red chilli, asafoetida powder, and a few curry leaves.

When the mustard seeds splutter, add the finely chopped green chillies, cooked rice, salt to taste, and sautéed coconut. Mix thoroughly. Sprinkle the powdered sesame seeds over the mixture.

Garnish with the sautéed cashew nuts. Serve hot.

OPPOSITE – *Coconut Rice (top left) and Lemon Rice (bottom right)*

LEMON RICE
Elumichampazha Sadam

PREPARATION TIME: 20 MIN. COOKING TIME: 35 MIN.
SERVES 4

1 cup (5 oz) long-grained rice
2 green chillies (chili peppers), finely chopped
a piece of fresh ginger (2 1/2 cm/1 in) long, finely chopped
3 tablespoons raw peanuts
1/4 teaspoon ground turmeric
salt to taste
juice of 2 lemons
coriander (Chinese parsley) leaves, chopped (to garnish)

FOR TEMPERING

2 teaspoons oil
1 teaspoon brown mustard seeds
1 teaspoon cumin seeds
1 teaspoon black gram dal (washed urad dal),
picked over and rinsed
1 teaspoon Bengal gram dal (yellow split peas,
chana dal), picked over and rinsed
1 red chilli (chili pepper), halved
1/2 teaspoon asafoetida powder
a few curry leaves

Method

Cook the rice and set aside.

TEMPERING: Heat 2 teaspoons oil in a heavy frying pan or skillet. Add the mustard seeds, cumin seeds, black gram dal, Bengal gram dal, halved red chilli, asafoetida powder, and a few curry leaves.

When the mustard seeds splutter, add the finely chopped green chillies, finely chopped ginger, and peanuts. Sauté this mixture for 2–3 minutes.

Add the cooked rice, ground turmeric, and salt to taste. Mix thoroughly. Remove from the heat and add the lemon juice.

Garnish with chopped coriander leaves. Serve hot.

To perk up ordinary Lemon Rice, dry-roast and powder a 1cm/1/2 in piece cinnamon bark, 2 whole cardamom pods, 2 teaspoons aniseed, 2 cloves, and 2 teaspoons poppy seeds. Sprinkle this masala into the rice just before turning off the heat and adding the lemon juice.

TAMARIND RICE
Pulliodarai

TO MAKE THE TAMARIND CHUTNEY

**PREPARATION TIME: 30 MIN. COOKING TIME: 30 MIN.
MAKES APPROX. 200 G (7 OZ)**

an orange-sized piece of tamarind pulp
3 cups (24 fl oz) hot water
salt to taste
1/2 teaspoon ground turmeric
2 tablespoons powdered jaggery

MASALA

2 tablespoons oil
1/2 cup (1 1/2 oz) coriander seeds
8 red chillies (chili peppers)
1/2 teaspoon asafoetida powder
1 teaspoon black peppercorns
1 teaspoon cumin seeds
1 teaspoon fenugreek seeds
1/2 teaspoon brown mustard seeds
*1 tablespoon Bengal gram dal (yellow split peas,
chana dal), picked over and rinsed*
*1 tablespoon black gram dal (washed urad dal),
picked over and rinsed*
a few curry leaves

GARNISH

1/2 cup (2 oz) white sesame seeds
1/4 coconut, grated (approx. 1/3 cup flaked coconut)

FOR TEMPERING

2 tablespoons sesame oil
10 red chillies (chili peppers)
2 teaspoons brown mustard seeds
*1 tablespoon Bengal gram dal (yellow split peas,
chana dal), picked over and rinsed*
a few curry leaves

Method

Soak the tamarind in 3 cups (24 fl oz) hot water for 15 minutes. Strain the tamarind water into another container, squeezing as much liquid as possible out of the tamarind pulp. Discard pulp. Set the juice aside.

MASALA: Heat 2 tablespoons oil in a heavy frying pan or skillet. Add the coriander seeds, 8 red chillies, asafoetida powder, black peppercorns, cumin seeds, fenugreek seeds, mustard seeds, Bengal gram dal, black gram dal, and a few curry leaves. Sauté for 2–3 minutes. Place mixture in an electric blender or food processor. Blend ingredients into a fine powder. Set aside

GARNISH: In a heavy saucepan, dry-roast the sesame seeds and the grated coconut for 5 minutes. Place in an electric blender or food processor. Blend ingredients into a fine powder and set aside for garnish.

TEMPERING: Heat 2 tablespoons sesame oil in a heavy saucepan. Add the 10 red chillies, and sauté until dark brown in colour. Add the mustard seeds, Bengal gram dal, and a few curry leaves.

When the mustard seeds splutter, add the tamarind juice, salt to taste, ground turmeric, and jaggery.

Simmer over a low heat until the mixture thickens to almost a jam consistency. Add all of the masala powder. Mix thoroughly. Add 2 tablespoons of the garnish powder. Blend thoroughly. Set aside the remaining powder for garnishing the rice.

TO MAKE THE RICE

**PREPARATION TIME: 10 MIN. COOKING TIME: 30 MIN.
SERVES 4**

1 cup (5 oz) long-grained rice
2 tablespoons sesame oil
1 teaspoon ground turmeric
salt to taste
2/3 cup (3 oz) roasted peanuts
3–4 tablespoons Tamarind Chutney (see above)
2 tablespoons garnish powder (see above)

FOR TEMPERING

1 tablespoon sesame oil
2 teaspoons brown mustard seeds
*1 tablespoon Bengal gram dal (yellow split peas,
chana dal), picked over and rinsed*
*1 tablespoon black gram dal (washed urad dal),
picked over and rinsed*
1 teaspoon asafoetida powder
a few curry leaves

Method

Cook the rice and spread on a platter to cool.

When the rice is cool, pour over the 2 tablespoons sesame oil. Add the ground turmeric and salt to taste. Mix thoroughly.

TEMPERING: Heat 1 tablespoon sesame oil in a heavy frying pan or skillet. Add the mustard seeds, Bengal gram dal, black gram dal, asafoetida powder, and a few curry leaves.

When the mustard seeds splutter, add roasted peanuts. Sauté for 2–3 minutes. Add this mixture to the rice.

Now add 3–4 tablespoons Tamarind Chutney. Mix thoroughly. Sprinkle the garnish powder (remaining from the chutney) over the rice. Stir thoroughly.

Serve with fried poppadoms or potato wafers.

The Tamarind Chutney used in this recipe will keep for months in a refrigerator. Store and use as required. To perk up the rice, you need only make the garnish powder fresh every time.

ABOVE – *Tamarind Rice with Tamarind Chutney*

GREEN PEA RICE
Pattani Sadam

PREPARATION TIME: 30 MIN. COOKING TIME: 30 MIN.
SERVES 4

1 cup (5 oz) long-grained rice
1 cup (6 oz) shelled green peas
1 small potato, peeled and finely chopped
2 small eggplants (aubergines), finely chopped
1 sweet pepper (capsicum), finely chopped
1 teaspoon ground turmeric
salt to taste

MASALA

2 teaspoons oil
3 tablespoons coriander seeds
½ teaspoon asafoetida powder
2 tablespoons black gram dal (washed urad dal),
picked over and rinsed
3 tablespoons Bengal gram dal (yellow split peas, chana dal),
picked over and rinsed
5 red chillies (chili peppers)
a marble-sized piece of tamarind pulp

FOR TEMPERING

3 tablespoons oil
2 teaspoons brown mustard seeds
1 teaspoon black gram dal (washed urad dal), picked over and rinsed
1 teaspoon Bengal gram dal (yellow split peas,
chana dal), picked over and rinsed
1 red chilli (chili pepper), halved
a few curry leaves

Method

Cook the rice and set aside to cool.

MASALA: Heat the oil in a heavy frying pan or skillet. Add coriander seeds, asafoetida powder, black gram dal, Bengal gram dal, and red chillies. Sauté for 2–3 minutes. Place in an electric blender or food processor. Add tamarind pulp. Blend to a fine powder.

TEMPERING: Heat the oil in a heavy saucepan. Add mustard seeds, dals, red chilli, and a few curry leaves.

When the mustard seeds splutter, add the vegetables. Cook over a low heat, adding water if necessary. Add masala powder, ground turmeric, and salt to taste. Sauté for 1–2 minutes.

Add rice and mix well. Serve hot.

MANGO RICE
Mangai Sadam

PREPARATION TIME: 20 MIN. COOKING TIME: 30 MIN.
SERVES 4

1 cup (5 oz) long-grained rice
4 tablespoons raw peanuts
salt to taste
a few curry leaves

MASALA

1½ teaspoons brown mustard seeds
½ teaspoon asafoetida powder
6 red chillies (chili peppers)
½ teaspoon ground turmeric
4 tablespoons grated fresh coconut or 5½ tablespoons
flaked coconut
1½ cups grated green mango

FOR TEMPERING

3 tablespoons oil
1 teaspoon brown mustard seeds
1 tablespoon Bengal gram dal (yellow split peas,
chana dal), picked over and rinsed
1 red chilli (chili pepper), halved
a few curry leaves

Method

Cook the rice and spread on a platter to cool. Set aside.

MASALA: Place mustard seeds, asafoetida powder, 6 red chillies, ground turmeric, and grated coconut in an electric blender or food processor. Add half the grated mango. Blend into a fine paste. Set aside.

TEMPERING: Heat the oil in a heavy frying pan or skillet. Add mustard seeds, Bengal gram dal, red chilli, and a few curry leaves.

When the mustard seeds splutter, add the peanuts. Once the dal is golden, add the remaining mango. Sauté for a few minutes over a medium heat, until the mango is cooked. Now add the masala. Cook until the raw smell disappears. Remove from heat and set aside.

When the rice is cool, add salt to taste and extra curry leaves. Stir in the masala little by little, until well blended.

Serve hot with fried poppadoms or potato wafers.

OPPOSITE – *Green Pea Rice (top left) and Mango Rice (bottom right)*

BLACK GRAM DAL RICE
Ulundu Sadam

PREPARATION TIME: 20 MIN. COOKING TIME: 30 MIN.
SERVES 4

1 cup (5 oz) long-grained rice
1 tablespoon ghee
2 tablespoons raw cashew nuts, halved (to garnish)
2 green chillies (chili peppers), finely chopped
salt to taste

DRY MASALA

2 tablespoons black gram dal (washed urad dal), picked over and rinsed
1¹/₂ teaspoons black peppercorns
2 tablespoons white sesame seeds (optional)
2 tablespoons grated copra*

FOR TEMPERING

2 tablespoons ghee
1 teaspoon brown mustard seeds
1 teaspoon black gram dal (washed urad dal), picked over and rinsed
1 teaspoon Bengal gram dal (yellow split peas, chana dal), picked over and rinsed
1 red chilli (chili pepper), slit sideways
¹/₂ teaspoon asafoetida powder
a few curry leaves

Method

Cook the rice and set aside.

MASALA: In a heavy saucepan, dry-roast the black gram dal, black peppercorns, sesame seeds, and grated copra, for about 5 minutes. Place in an electric blender or food processor. Blend to a fine powder. Set aside.

Heat 1 tablespoon ghee in a heavy frying pan or skillet. Sauté 2 tablespoons halved cashew nuts until golden in colour. Set aside.

TEMPERING: Heat 2 tablespoons ghee. Add mustard seeds, black gram dal, Bengal gram dal, slit red chilli, asafoetida powder, and a few curry leaves.

When the mustard seeds splutter, add green chillies. Sauté for 2–3 minutes. Add rice and mix well. Now add salt to taste and masala powder. Mix well. Garnish with cashews.

Serve hot with poppadoms or potato wafers.

*If copra is unavailable, dry-roasted grated or flaked coconut may be substituted. However, if fresh coconut is used, the dish will spoil more quickly.

MUSTARD SEED RICE
Kadugu Sadam

PREPARATION TIME: 15 MIN. COOKING TIME: 30 MIN.
SERVES 4

1 cup (5 oz) long-grained rice
3 tablespoons raw peanuts
salt to taste

PASTE

1 tablespoon brown mustard seeds
¹/₂ coconut, grated (approx. ¹/₂ cup flaked coconut)
4 red chillies (chili peppers)
¹/₂ teaspoon ground turmeric
¹/₂ teaspoon asafoetida powder
a marble-sized piece of tamarind pulp
a little water

FOR TEMPERING

1 tablespoon ghee
1 teaspoon brown mustard seeds
1¹/₂ teaspoons black gram dal (washed urad dal), picked over and rinsed
1¹/₂ teaspoons Bengal gram dal (yellow split peas), picked over and rinsed
1 red chilli (chili pepper), halved
a few curry leaves

Method

Cook the rice and set aside.

PASTE: Place mustard seeds, grated coconut, red chillies, ground turmeric, asafoetida powder, and tamarind pulp in an electric blender or food processor. Add very little water. Blend into a fine paste. Set aside.

TEMPERING: Heat 1 tablespoon ghee in a heavy frying pan or skillet. Add mustard seeds, black gram dal, Bengal gram dal, halved red chilli, and a few curry leaves.

When the mustard seeds splutter, add the peanuts. Sauté for 2–3 minutes. Now add the paste. Sauté until the raw smell disappears. Lastly, add the cooked rice, and salt to taste. Stir thoroughly.

Serve hot.

OPPOSITE – *Black Gram Dal Rice (top left) and Mustard Seed Rice (bottom right)*

Spicy Sambar Rice

Bissi Bele Hulli Anna

PREPARATION TIME: 30 MIN. COOKING TIME: 45 MIN.
SERVES 6

1 cup (6 oz) red gram dal (pigeon peas, toor dal), picked over and rinsed
1 cup (5 oz) long-grained rice
4½ cups (36 fl oz) water
a lime-sized piece of tamarind pulp
2 cups (16 fl oz) hot water
½ cup (approx. 4 oz) peeled and chopped golden shallots*
1 sweet pepper (capsicum), finely chopped
1 small eggplant (aubergine), finely chopped
2 tablespoons green peas (optional)
1 potato, finely diced
½ teaspoon ground turmeric
salt to taste
6 tablespoons ghee
coriander (Chinese parsley) leaves, chopped (to garnish)

PASTE

4 teaspoons oil
10 red chillies (chili peppers)
3 tablespoons coriander seeds
a piece of cinnamon bark (2½ cm/1 in long)
3 teaspoons Bengal gram dal (yellow split peas,
chana dal), picked over and rinsed
1½ teaspoons poppy seeds
4 cloves
½ teaspoon fenugreek seeds
½ coconut, grated (approx. ¾ cup flaked coconut)
1 teaspoon asafoetida powder
a little water

DRY MASALA

3 tablespoons fried gram dal**
1½ teaspoons poppy seeds
3 teaspoons uncooked rice
2–3 tablespoons grated fresh coconut or
2½–4 tablespoons flaked coconut

FOR TEMPERING

2 tablespoons oil
1 teaspoon brown mustard seeds
1 teaspoon cumin seeds
1 tablespoon black gram dal (washed urad dal)
1 tablespoon Bengal gram dal (yellow split peas,
chana dal), picked over and rinsed
1 red chilli (chili pepper), halved
a few curry leaves

Method

Rinse red gram dal well. Place in a heavy saucepan. Add the rice. Cover with 4½ cups (36 fl oz) water and bring to the boil. When boiling, cover the pan with a lid. Simmer gently for 30–45 minutes. When cooked, set aside in the saucepan so that the heat is not lost. Do not drain.

PASTE: Heat the oil in a heavy frying pan or skillet. Add red chillies, coriander seeds, cinnamon bark, Bengal gram dal, poppy seeds, cloves, fenugreek seeds, grated coconut, and asafoetida powder. Sauté for 2–3 minutes. Place in an electric blender or food processor. Add very little water. Blend into a fine paste.

MASALA: In a heavy saucepan, dry-roast fried gram dal, poppy seeds, uncooked rice and grated coconut, for about 5 minutes. Place in an electric blender or food processor. Blend ingredients into a fine powder.

Soak the tamarind in 2 cups (16 fl oz) hot water for 15 minutes. Strain the tamarind water into another container, squeezing as much liquid as possible out of the pulp. Discard pulp. Set the juice aside.

TEMPERING: Heat the oil in a heavy saucepan. Add mustard seeds, cumin seeds, black gram dal, Bengal gram dal, halved red chilli, and a few curry leaves.

When the mustard seeds splutter, add chopped shallots. Sauté for 2–3 minutes. Now add the sweet pepper, eggplant, green peas (if used), and potato. Sauté until the vegetables are partly cooked. Add tamarind juice, ground turmeric, and salt to taste. Cook until the vegetables are tender. Add the paste and cook for a few minutes more.

Using the same saucepan, gradually add the undrained rice and dal mixture to the sambar. Take care that no lumps form. Simmer on a low heat. Now add 6 tablespoons ghee. Cook until well blended. Lastly, add the dry masala. Remove from heat. Garnish with chopped coriander leaves.

Serve hot with fried poppadoms.

*If shallots are unavailable, use spring onions instead.
**Fried gram dal is roasted and puffed Bengal gram dal (yellow split peas, chana dal). Use dry-roasted Bengal gram dal if this is unavailable.

This rich, spicy rice is a meal in itself. For extra flavour, add hot ghee with sautéed cashews and curry leaves before serving.

RICE PONGAL
Ven Pongal

**PREPARATION TIME: 10 MIN. COOKING TIME: 1 HR 15 MIN.
SERVES 4**

1 teaspoon cumin seeds
1 teaspoon black peppercorns
2 tablespoons raw cashew nuts
2 tablespoons ghee
1 cup (5 oz) long-grained rice
½ cup (3 oz) green gram dal (split mung beans,
moong dal), picked over and rinsed
½ teaspoon ground turmeric

4½ cups (36 fl oz) water
4 tablespoons ghee (extra)
2 tablespoons oil
1 teaspoon asafoetida powder
a piece of fresh ginger (2½ cm/1 in long), grated
a few curry leaves
salt to taste
2 tablespoons grated fresh coconut or 2½ tablespoons
flaked coconut (optional)

Method

Place cumin seeds and black peppercorns in an electric blender or food processor. Blend into a coarse powder. Split the cashews in half. Sauté in 2 tablespoons of ghee until golden in colour. Set both aside.

In a heavy saucepan, dry-roast the rice and green gram dal separately, about 5 minutes each. Wash both rice and green gram dal well. Mix together and place in a saucepan. Add ground turmeric and 4½ cups (36 fl oz) water. Bring to the boil. Boil for 15 minutes. Reduce the heat and cover pan. Simmer for 30–45 minutes until soft. When cooked, set aside. Do not drain.

Heat extra ghee and oil in a heavy frying pan or skillet. Add cumin seed/peppercorn powder, asafoetida powder, grated ginger and a few curry leaves. Sauté for 1 minute. Add undrained rice and dal, salt to taste, and coconut. Mix well. If necessary, add ½ cup (4 fl oz) water.

Garnish with sautéed cashews. Serve hot with any coconut chutney or Spicy Tamarind Sambar (p. 10).

If you wish to cut down on fat, use only 3½ cups (28 fl oz) water. Add 1 cup (8 fl oz) milk, and cook the rice and dal as usual. You need only use half the quantity of extra ghee stipulated in the recipe. This makes a very soft pongal.

TOMATO RICE
Thakkali Sadam

PREPARATION TIME: 20 MIN. COOKING TIME: 30 MIN.
SERVES 4

1 cup (5 oz) long-grained rice
4 large tomatoes, chopped
salt to taste
½ teaspoon ground turmeric
2 green chillies (chili peppers), finely chopped
2–3 medium onions, finely chopped

MASALA

2 teaspoons oil
6 red chillies (chili peppers)
2 teaspoons coriander seeds
¼ teaspoon fenugreek seeds
3 teaspoons Bengal gram dal (yellow split peas,
chana dal), picked over and rinsed
1 teaspoon black gram dal (washed urad dal), picked over and rinsed
½ teaspoon asafoetida powder
2 tablespoons grated copra*

FOR TEMPERING

2 tablespoons oil
2 teaspoons ghee

1 teaspoon brown mustard seeds
2 tablespoons raw peanuts
a few curry leaves

Method

Cook the rice. Spread on a platter to cool.

Blend chopped tomatoes in an electric blender or food processor. Strain the juice and set aside.

MASALA: Heat 2 teaspoons oil in a heavy frying pan or skillet. Add red chillies, coriander seeds, fenugreek seeds, Bengal gram dal, black gram dal, asafoetida powder, and grated copra. Sauté for 2–3 minutes. Blend to a fine paste in an electric blender or food processor.

To a heavy saucepan, add the tomato juice, salt to taste, and ground turmeric. Simmer until mixture thickens. Add masala paste and mix thoroughly. Set aside.

TEMPERING: Heat 2 tablespoons oil and 2 tablespoons ghee in a heavy saucepan. Add the mustard seeds, peanuts, and a few curry leaves.

When the mustard seeds splutter, add the green chillies and onions. Sauté for 2–3 minutes until golden in colour. Add the rice and tomato concentrate. Mix thoroughly. Serve hot with fried poppadoms or potato wafers.

*If copra is unavailable, dry-roasted grated or flaked coconut may be substituted. However, if fresh coconut is used the dish will spoil more quickly.

CURD RICE
Thair Sadam

PREPARATION TIME: 30 MIN. COOKING TIME: 20 MIN.
SERVES 4

1 cup (5 oz) long-grained rice
1 small green mango, peeled and finely chopped (optional)
1 cucumber, peeled and finely chopped
salt to taste
2 green chillies (chili peppers), finely chopped
a piece of fresh ginger (2½ cm/1 in long), finely chopped
coriander (Chinese parsley) leaves, finely chopped
2 cups (16 fl oz) plain yogurt (see p. 136)
½ cup (4 fl oz) milk
1 carrot, peeled and grated (to garnish)

FOR TEMPERING

2 teaspoons oil
1 teaspoon brown mustard seeds
2 teaspoons black gram dal (washed urad dal),
picked over and rinsed
2 teaspoons Bengal gram dal (yellow split peas,
chana dal), picked over and rinsed
1 red chilli (chili pepper), halved
¹/₂ teaspoon asafoetida powder
a few curry leaves

Method

Cook the rice as usual, then mash into a bowl using a sieve or strainer. Add the mango, cucumber, and salt to taste. Mix thoroughly

TEMPERING: Heat the oil in a heavy frying pan or skillet. Add mustard seeds, black gram dal, Bengal gram dal, halved red chilli, asafoetida powder, and a few curry leaves

When the mustard seeds splutter, add mixture to the rice. Add green chillies, ginger and most of the chopped coriander. Mix thoroughly. Add the yogurt and milk. Mix thoroughly again.

Garnish with carrot and extra coriander. Serve at room temperature or slightly chilled.

ABOVE – *Tomato Rice (top left) and Curd Rice (bottom right)*
PREVIOUS PAGE – *Rice Pongal (top left) and*
Spicy Sambar Rice (bottom right)

DAL POWDER
Parupu Podi

PREPARATION TIME: 10 MIN. COOKING TIME: 10 MIN.
MAKES 200 G (7 OZ)

1 cup (5 oz) red gram dal (pigeon peas, toor dal),
picked over and rinsed
1 tablespoon Bengal gram dal (yellow split peas,
chana dal), picked over and rinsed
1 tablespoon black gram dal (washed urad dal)
1 tablespoon ghee
$^1/_2$ tablespoon black peppercorns
1 teaspoon cumin seeds
5 red chillies (chili peppers)
$^1/_2$ teaspoon asafoetida powder
salt to taste

Method

In a heavy saucepan, dry-roast the three dals over a low heat, for
about 4–5 minutes. Set aside.

Heat ghee in the same pan. Add black peppercorns, cumin
seeds, red chillies, and asafoetida powder. Sauté for 2–3 minutes.
Blend into a powder in an electric blender or food processor with
roasted dals. Add salt to taste.

Serve with plain hot rice and ghee.

Store in an airtight container and use as required.

SESAME SEED POWDER
Ellu Podi

PREPARATION TIME: 15 MIN. COOKING TIME: 5 MIN.
MAKES 200 G (7 OZ)

4 teaspoons oil
1 cup (4 oz) white sesame seeds
$^1/_2$ cup (approx. 1 oz) grated copra*
10–12 red chillies (chili peppers)
1 teaspoon asafoetida powder
salt to taste

Method

Heat the oil in a heavy frying pan or skillet. Add the sesame seeds,
grated copra, red chillies and asafoetida powder. Sauté for 2–3
minutes. Place mixture in an electric blender or food processor.
Blend ingredients into a coarse powder. Add salt to taste.

Serve with plain hot rice and ghee.

**If copra is unavailable, dry-roasted grated or flaked coconut may
be substituted. If fresh coconut is used, this powder will not keep for
more than 3–4 days, slightly longer if kept in the refrigerator.*

Store in an airtight container and use as required.

PEANUT POWDER
Verkadalai Podi

PREPARATION TIME: 10 MIN. COOKING TIME: 10 MIN.
MAKES 200 G (7 OZ)

¹/₂ cup (2 oz) white sesame seeds
2 teaspoons oil
15 red chillies (chili peppers)
1 teaspoon asafoetida powder
2 cups (10 oz) peanuts, roasted
salt to taste

Method

Dry-roast the sesame seeds in a heavy saucepan, for about 5 minutes. Set aside.

Heat 2 teaspoons oil in the same pan. Add the red chillies and asafoetida powder. Sauté for 2–3 minutes.

Place this mixture in an electric blender or food processor. Add the roasted sesame seeds. Blend ingredients into a fine powder. Lastly, add the roasted peanuts. Blend coarsely and add salt to taste.

Serve with plain hot rice and ghee.

This powder is meant to be nutty and crunchy. Do not powder the peanuts too finely.

Store in an airtight container and use as required.

COCONUT POWDER
Thengai Podi

PREPARATION TIME: 15 MIN. COOKING TIME: 10 MIN.
MAKES 200 G (7 OZ)

¹/₂ coconut, grated (approx. ³/₄ cup flaked coconut)
2 tablespoons red gram dal (pigeon peas, toor dal),
picked over and rinsed
2 tablespoons Bengal gram dal (yellow split peas,
chana dal), picked over and rinsed
1 teaspoon oil
8 red chillies (chili peppers)
¹/₂ teaspoon asafoetida powder
salt to taste

Method

Dry-roast the grated coconut in a heavy saucepan until golden. Set aside. In the same pan, dry-roast the red gram dal and Bengal gram dal together, over a low heat, for about 5 minutes. Set aside.

Heat the oil in the same pan. Add the red chillies and asafoetida powder. Sauté for 2–3 minutes. Place in an electric blender or food processor. Add roasted coconut and dals. Blend to a coarse powder. Add salt to taste.

Serve with plain hot rice and ghee.

This powder will keep for 3–4 days, longer if refrigerated. Store in an airtight container and use as required.

CURRY LEAF POWDER
Karivepilai Podi

PREPARATION TIME: 20 MIN. COOKING TIME: 7 MIN.
MAKES 200 G (7 OZ)

1 large bunch of curry leaves (30–35 leaves)
2 teaspoons oil
1 cup (3 oz) coriander seeds
1 tablespoon black peppercorns
1 tablespoon cumin seeds
1/2 tablespoon fenugreek seeds
1/2 tablespoon brown mustard seeds
1 tablespoon black gram dal (washed urad dal),
picked over and rinsed
1 tablespoon Bengal gram dal (yellow split peas,
chana dal), picked over and rinsed
1 teaspoon asafoetida powder
2 tablespoons powdered jaggery
a marble-sized piece of tamarind pulp
salt to taste

Method

Dry-roast the curry leaves in a heavy saucepan for 2–3 minutes. Set aside.

Heat 2 teaspoons oil in the same pan. Add coriander seeds, black peppercorns, cumin seeds, fenugreek seeds, mustard seeds, black gram dal, Bengal gram dal, and asafoetida powder. Sauté for 2–3 minutes. Place this mixture in an electric blender or food processor.

Add the roasted curry leaves, jaggery, tamarind pulp, and salt to taste. Blend ingredients into a fine powder.

Serve with plain hot rice and ghee.

Store in an airtight container and use as required.

CHUTNEY POWDER
Chutney Podi

PREPARATION TIME: 15 MIN. COOKING TIME: 10 MIN.
MAKES 200 G (7 OZ)

1/2 cup (3 oz) Bengal gram dal (yellow split peas,
chana dal), picked over and rinsed
1/2 cup (3 oz) black gram dal (washed urad dal),
picked over and rinsed
1/2 cup (approx. 1 oz) grated copra*
2 teaspoons oil
10–12 red chillies (chili peppers)
1/2 teaspoon asafoetida powder
1 tablespoon powdered jaggery
a marble-sized piece of tamarind pulp
a few curry leaves
salt to taste

Method

Dry-roast the Bengal gram dal, black gram dal, and grated copra in a heavy saucepan, for about 5 minutes. Remove from the pan and set aside.

Heat the oil in the same pan. Add the red chillies and asafoetida powder. Sauté for 2–3 minutes. Place in an electric blender or food processor. Add roasted dals and copra, and the jaggery, tamarind pulp, and a few curry leaves. Blend into a fine powder. Add salt to taste.

Serve with plain hot rice and ghee.

If copra is unavailable, dry-roasted grated or flaked coconut may be substituted. If fresh coconut is used, this powder will only keep for 2–3 days, slightly longer if refrigerated. Store in an airtight container and use as required.

GREEN PLANTAIN CRUMBLE
Vazhakkai Podi

PREPARATION TIME: 20 MIN. COOKING TIME: 20 MIN.
SERVES 4

a little oil
3 raw green plantains
salt to taste
1 tablespoon oil (extra)

2 tablespoons Bengal gram dal (yellow split peas,
chana dal), picked over and rinsed
2 tablespoons black gram dal (washed urad dal),
picked over and rinsed
1 tablespoon red gram dal (pigeon peas, toor dal),
picked over and rinsed
6–8 red chillies (chili peppers)
¹⁄₂ teaspoon asafoetida powder

Method

Smear oil on the skin of the plantains. Either roast directly over a naked flame or grill (broil) until cooked (the skin will turn black). When cool, skin the plantains and grate into a bowl. Add salt to taste. Set aside.

Heat 1 tablespoon oil in a heavy frying pan or skillet. Add the Bengal gram dal, black gram dal, red gram dal, asafoetida powder, and red chillies. Sauté for 2–3 minutes. Place this mixture in an electric blender or food processor. Blend ingredients into a fine powder.

Mix the grated plantain with the powder in a heavy saucepan over a low heat, until thoroughly blended.

Serve with rice or as a side dish.

If you don't much care for the roasted, smoky flavour of the plantains, boil them in their skins instead of roasting or grilling. Peel, grate and cook as above.

For Potato Crumble, boil, peel and mash the potatoes. Stir in the powder and sauté until well blended. This version is equally delicious.

SNACKS

Snacks, commonly called 'tiffins', occupy a very special place in South Indian cooking. Crunchy, soft, spicy, sweet or fiery hot, snacks can be steamed, shallow-fried or deep-fried. Serve them as afternoon treats or along with a meal.

~

For nibblers, these delicious snacks wil be utterly irresistible. More often than not, of course, they are a complete meal in themselves. In fact, in South India, any time is tiffin time.

ORDINARY DOSAI

Dosai

PREPARATION TIME: 24 HRS; COOKING TIME: 45 MIN.
MAKES 20

3 cups (18 oz) parboiled (converted) rice
water for soaking
1 cup (8 fl oz) water
1 cup (6 oz) black gram dal (washed urad dal),
picked over and rinsed
2 teaspoons fenugreek seeds
2 cups (16 fl oz) water
½ cup (4 fl oz) water (extra)
salt to taste
oil for shallow-frying

Method

Soak parboiled rice in twice its volume of water for at least 6 hours. Drain completely. Make a smooth batter of the rice in an electric blender or food processor, gradually adding 1 cup (8 fl oz) water. At the same time, soak black gram dal and fenugreek seeds in 2 cups (16 fl oz) water, also for 6 hours. Drain completely. Blend to a smooth batter in an electric blender or food processor, gradually adding ½ cup (4 fl oz) water.

Combine the two batters, add salt to taste, and set aside for at least 12 hours, until the batter ferments. Use a large container as the batter will increase in volume. It should become a mass of tiny bubbles. Once fermented, add more water, just enough to make a batter of thick pouring consistency.

TO PREPARE TAWA (GRIDDLE): Heat the tawa or griddle.* To test if it is hot enough for use, sprinkle a few drops of water over the surface. If the water sizzles, the tawa is ready for use. Smear a little oil on the tawa. (Do not use too much as the batter will not spread evenly.) When the oil smokes, lower the heat slightly.

TO MAKE DOSAIS: Pour a ladleful of batter over the tawa. Spread quickly, using a continuous spiral motion, spreading outwards until dosai measures about 15 cm (6 in) in diameter.

Pour 1 teaspoon of oil around the edges. Increase the heat. Cook for 2–3 minutes, until the bottom of the dosai is golden. Turn over, carefully lifting the edges as you would a pancake. Cook the second side until golden.

Serve hot with Coconut Chutney (see p. 122).

If you do not have a tawa or griddle, use a cast-iron frying pan or skillet. Sprinkle water on the tawa in between making dosais to prevent it overheating. If dosais repeatedly stick to the tawa, rub it with a halved potato, eggplant (aubergine) or onion dipped in oil. The leftover batter can be stored in the refrigerator for a couple of days.

Keep a separate tawa for making dosais. After cleaning, smear the surface with a little oil to prevent rust, and store.

SEMOLINA DOSAI

Rava Dosai

PREPARATION TIME: 2 HRS 15 MIN. COOKING TIME: 30 MIN.
MAKES 15–20

1 cup (4 oz) plain (all-purpose) flour
1 cup (5 oz) semolina
1 cup (4 oz) rice flour
salt to taste
2 teaspoons cumin seeds
3–4 green chillies (chili peppers), finely chopped
1 cup (8 fl oz) plain yogurt (see p. 136)
a few curry leaves
1 small bunch of coriander (Chinese parsley) leaves, finely chopped
water as required
oil for shallow-frying

Method

Mix plain flour, semolina, and rice flour in a bowl, Add salt to taste, cumin seeds, green chillies, plain yogurt, curry leaves, and coriander. Combine thoroughly. Add enough water to form a stiff dough. Set aside for at least 2 hours. Add water to make a batter of thin pouring consistency (thinner than ordinary dosai batter.)

TO PREPARE TAWA: See Ordinary Dosai (opposite).

TO MAKE DOSAIS: Pour a ladleful of batter onto the outer edges of the tawa. Continue to pour inwards, using a circular motion, to make a dosai 12–15 cm (5–6 in) in diameter.* Smooth the surface gently with the back of a ladle to remove lumps. Pour 1 teaspoon of oil around the edges. Cook both sides until golden, as you would a pancake. This dosai will have small holes over its surface.

Serve hot with Coconut Chutney (see p. 122).

If you find it difficult to pour the batter inwards, pour as for Ordinary Dosai (opposite), but using slightly thicker batter.

For Onion Rava Dosai, add a chopped onion to the batter.

Also, although thinner and lighter than Masala Dosai, Semolina Masala Dosai is equally tempting.

OPPOSITE – *Ordinary Dosai (centre) and Semolina Dosai (bottom right), served with Coconut Chutney (top left)*

Masala Dosai

PREPARATION TIME: 24 HRS. COOKING TIME: 1 HOUR
MAKES 20–25

1 quantity dosai batter (see p. 84)
1 quantity Potato Masala (see p. 43)
oil for shallow-frying
coconut chutney (see Coconut Chutney 1, p. 122)
200 g (7 oz) cooking butter

Method

Prepare the dosai batter as given for Ordinary Dosai and the Potato Masala as given in the recipe. Set aside.

TO PREPARE TAWA: Heat the tawa or griddle. Sprinkle a few drops of water onto it. If the water sizzles, the tawa is ready for use. Smear a little oil on the tawa. When the oil smokes, lower the heat under the tawa slightly.

TO MAKE DOSAIS: Pour a ladleful of dosai batter onto the tawa and spread quickly, using a continuous spiral motion, until the dosai is about 15 cm (6 in) in diameter. Pour a teaspoon of oil all around the edge of the dosai.

Increase the heat and cook for a couple of minutes, until the bottom of the dosai is golden brown in colour. Remove the dosai from the pan and set aside. One side only of the dosai is cooked when making Masala Dosai. Continue making dosais until all the batter is used.

Taking one of the dosais, spread 1 tablespoon of coconut chutney on one half of one side only. Spread 1½ tablespoons of the Potato Masala over the coconut chutney. Fold the dosai over as you would an omelette. Sprinkle butter on top of the dosai and shallow-fry both sides until golden. Continue this process until all dosais are used.

Serve hot with Coconut Chutney (p. 122) and Small Onion Sambar (p. 2).

If you like a fresh, minty flavour, add a few sprigs of fresh mint leaves to the Potato Masala before spreading on the dosais.

ABOVE RIGHT – *Spread 1 tablespoon of the coconut chutney on one half only of the dosai.*
MIDDLE RIGHT – *Spread 1¹/₂ tablespoons of the Potato Masala over the coconut chutney.*
BOTTOM RIGHT – *Fold the dosai over. Sprinkle the butter on top of the dosai and shallow-fry both sides until golden.*
OPPOSITE – *Masala Dosai*

OOTHAPPAM

PREPARATION TIME: 20 MIN. COOKING TIME: 30 MIN.
MAKES 6–8

2 cups leftover sour dosai batter (see p. 84)
1 onion, finely chopped
1 tomato, finely chopped
1–2 green chillies (chili peppers), finely chopped
1 small bunch of coriander (Chinese parsley) leaves,
finely chopped
oil for shallow-frying

Method

Mix the finely chopped onion, tomato, green chillies and coriander leaves together. Set aside.

TO PREPARE TAWA: See Ordinary Dosai (p. 84).

TO MAKE OOTHAPPAMS: Pour a ladleful of batter onto the tawa to make a thick dosai (½ cm/¼ in). Do not spread the batter out thinly. Pour 1 teaspoon of oil around the edges of the oothappam.

Take a tablespoon of the vegetable mixture. Sprinkle evenly over the oothappam. Cook until the bottom of the oothappam is golden in colour. Turn over carefully, and cook the other side until golden.

Serve hot with chutney.

Fluffy oothappams are normally made from leftover sour dosai batter. If freshly fermented batter is used, add plain yogurt (see p. 136) — ¼ cup (2 fl oz) yogurt to 2 cups (16 fl oz) fresh batter — and then make the oothappams.

A sprinkling of 1 tablespoon cheese, 1 tablespoon finely chopped sweet pepper (capsicum), and 2 tablespoons grated fresh coconut (2½ tablespoons flaked coconut) makes a delicious variation.

Oothappams topped with vegetables are as tasty as pizzas.

RAGI DOSAI

PREPARATION TIME: 2 HRS 15 MIN. COOKING TIME: 30 MIN.
MAKES 15–20

2 cups (8 oz) ragi flour*
1/2 cup (2 oz) rice flour
salt to taste
1 bunch of coriander (Chinese parsley) leaves,
finely chopped
3–4 green chillies (chili peppers), finely chopped
1 onion, finely chopped (optional)
1/2 cup (4 fl oz) plain yogurt (see p. 130)
water
oil for shallow-frying

FOR TEMPERING

2 teaspoons oil
1 teaspoon brown mustard seeds
1 teaspoon cumin seeds
1/2 teaspoon asafoetida powder
a few curry leaves

Method

Sift the ragi flour, rice flour, and salt to taste into a bowl. Add the coriander leaves, green chillies, onion (if used), and plain yogurt. Combine thoroughly. Now add just enough water to form a batter of thin pouring consistency. Set aside for 2 hours.

TEMPERING: Heat 2 teaspoons oil in a heavy frying pan or skillet. Add the mustard seeds, cumin seeds, asafoetida powder, and a few curry leaves.

When the mustard seeds splutter, add this seasoning to the batter.

TO PREPARE TAWA: See Ordinary Dosai (p. 84).

TO MAKE DOSAIS: See Semolina Dosai (p. 84).

Cook both sides until golden in colour, as you would a pancake. Serve hot with chutney.

*Ragi flour is milled from a red grain that is widely cultivated in South India (Eleusine coracana gaertu). It may be available in Indian markets and Asian food stores. There are no suitable substitutes.

If you do not have a tawa or griddle, use a cast-iron frying pan or skillet. If you find it difficult to pour the batter inwards rather than outwards, pour it as you would for Ordinary Dosai (p. 84), but make sure the batter is slightly thicker or you won't get the desired result.

WHEAT FLOUR DOSAI
Godumai Dosai

PREPARATION TIME: 10 MIN. COOKING TIME: 40 MIN.
MAKES 12

2 cups (10 oz) whole-wheat (wholemeal) flour
1 cup (4 oz) rice flour
1/2 cup (4 fl oz) sour buttermilk*
water as required
2 green chillies (chili peppers), finely chopped
1 small bunch of coriander (Chinese parsley) leaves, finely chopped
salt to taste
oil for shallow-frying

FOR TEMPERING

1 1/2 teaspoons oil
1/2 teaspoon brown mustard seeds
1/2 teaspoon cumin seeds
1/4 teaspoon asafoetida powder
a few curry leaves

Method

Sift the whole-wheat flour and rice flour together into a bowl. Add sour buttermilk and combine well. Now add sufficient water to make a batter of pouring consistency. Add finely chopped chillies and coriander leaves.

TEMPERING: Heat 1 1/2 teaspoons oil in a heavy frying pan or skillet. Add the mustard seeds, cumin seeds, asafoetida powder, and a few curry leaves.

When the mustard seeds splutter, add this seasoning to the dosai batter. Add salt to taste, and mix thoroughly.

TO PREPARE TAWA: See Ordinary Dosai (p. 84).

TO MAKE DOSAIS: See Semolina Dosai (p. 84).

Cook both sides until golden in colour, as you would a pancake. Serve hot with Coconut Chutney (p. 122).

*If you do not have any sour buttermilk, add 1 teaspoon malt vinegar to ordinary buttermilk and use as instructed.

If you do not have a tawa or griddle, use a cast-iron frying pan or skillet. If you find it difficult to pour the batter inwards rather than outwards, pour it as you would for Ordinary Dosai (p. 84), but use slightly thicker batter or you won't get the desired result.

OPPOSITE – *Oothappam (bottom left), with Wheat Flour Dosai and Ragi Dosai (top right)*

JAGGERY DOSAI
Vella Dosai

**PREPARATION TIME: 30 MIN. COOKING TIME: 30 MIN.
MAKES 15–20**

*1 cup (approx. 6 oz) powdered jaggery
1 cup (8 fl oz) water
2 cups (10 oz) whole-wheat (wholemeal) flour
1 cup (4 oz) rice flour
oil for shallow-frying*

Method

In a heavy saucepan, heat jaggery and water. Simmer over a low heat, until thoroughly blended. Remove from heat, strain and cool. Now sift whole-wheat flour and rice flour into bowl. Make a well in the centre and add jaggery syrup. Combine thoroughly to make a batter of thin pouring consistency. Add water if necessary.

To Prepare Tawa: See Ordinary Dosai (p. 84).

To Make Dosais: See Ordinary Dosai (p. 84).

Serve dosais hot with a dollop of butter on top. For a sweet and sour flavour, serve with Instant Mango Pickle (p. 128).

This crisp dosai will be brown in colour, rather than golden, because of the jaggery it contains.

DAL DOSAI
Adai

**PREPARATION TIME: 2 HRS 30 MIN. COOKING TIME: 45 MIN.
MAKES 12**

*1/2 cup (3 oz) black gram dal (washed urad dal),
picked over and rinsed
1/2 cup (3 oz) red gram dal (pigeon peas, toor dal),
picked over and rinsed
1/2 cup (3 oz) Bengal gram dal (yellow split peas, chana dal),
picked over and rinsed
1 cup (5 oz) uncooked long-grain rice
4–6 red chillies (chili peppers)
2 cups (16 fl oz) water
a little water (extra)
salt to taste
4 tablespoons grated fresh coconut or 5 1/2 tablespoons
flaked coconut
1 large onion, finely chopped*

*1 bunch of coriander (Chinese parsley) leaves, chopped
1/2 teaspoon asafoetida powder
oil for shallow-frying*

Method

Soak black gram dal, red gram dal, Bengal gram dal, rice and red chillies in 2 cups (16 fl oz) water for 2 hours. Drain completely. Place mixture in an electric blender or food processor. Blend into a coarse paste, adding a little extra water only if necessary. Add salt to taste, grated coconut, onion, coriander leaves, and asafoetida powder. Combine thoroughly.

To Prepare Tawa: See Ordinary Dosai (p. 84).

To Make Dosais: Pour a ladleful of batter into the centre of the tawa. Spread outwards as you would an ordinary dosai, as thinly as possible. Make a hole in the centre of the dosai, Pour 1 teaspoon of oil in the centre and around the edges. Cook until golden brown on both sides, as you would a pancake. Shallow-fry until golden and crisp.

Serve hot with Coconut Chutney (p. 122).

For those with a hot palate, serve with Dosai Chilli Powder (p. 139). This dosai also tastes scrumptious with powdered jaggery and a dollop of butter sprinkled over the top.

Deep-fry the leftover batter as you would for pakoras (p. 105). These fritters are known as kunukkus. Drop spoonfuls of batter into the oil and fry till golden in colour.

GREEN GRAM DOSAI
Passhirattu

**PREPARATION TIME: 1 HOUR; COOKING TIME: 30 MIN.
MAKES 10**

*2 cups (12 oz) green gram dal (split mung beans,
moong dal), picked over and rinsed*
*1/2 cup (3 oz) uncooked long-grain rice
2 cups (16 fl oz) water
5 green chillies (chili peppers)
a little water (extra)
salt to taste
1/4 teaspoon asafoetida powder
1 large onion, finely chopped
2 tablespoons grated fresh coconut or
2 1/2 tablespoons flaked coconut (optional)
1 potato, boiled and mashed (optional)*

1 bunch of coriander (Chinese parsley) leaves,
finely chopped
oil for shallow-frying

Method

Wash the green gram dal well. Soak with rice in 2 cups (16 fl oz) water for 45 minutes. Drain completely. Place in an electric blender or food processor. Add green chillies. Blend into a coarse paste, adding a little extra water if necessary. Place batter in a mixing bowl. Add salt to taste, asafoetida powder, onion, grated coconut and mashed potato if you wish, and coriander leaves. Combine well to make a batter of thick dropping consistency.

TO PREPARE TAWA: See Ordinary Dosai (p. 84).
TO MAKE DOSAIS: See Dal Dosai (opposite).
  Serve hot with Coconut Chutney (p. 122).

*Use whole green gram with the husk (whole mung beans, sabat moong) for a wholesome and nutritious variation. In this case, soak the beans and rice for 3–4 hours.

POTATO DOSAI
Urulaikizhangu Dosai

PREPARATION TIME: 45 MIN. COOKING TIME: 30 MIN.
MAKES 10–15

2 large potatoes
1 cup (4 oz) rice flour, sifted
1/2 cup (4 fl oz) plain yogurt (see p. 136)
2 green chillies (chili peppers), finely chopped
1 small bunch of coriander (Chinese parsley) leaves, finely chopped
salt to taste
water as required
oil for shallow-frying

Method

Boil the potatoes in their jackets, peel and mash well.

In a mixing bowl, blend the mashed potatoes, sifted rice flour, yogurt, finely chopped green chillies, and coriander leaves. Add salt to taste. Mix well. Now add sufficient water to form a batter of pouring consistency.

TO PREPARE TAWA: See Ordinary Dosai (p. 84).
TO MAKE DOSAIS: See Ordinary Dosai (p. 84).
Serve hot with chutney.

If you do not have a tawa or griddle, use a cast-iron frying pan or skillet.

SPICY DOSAI
Kara Dosai

PREPARATION TIME: 2 HRS 30 MIN. COOKING TIME: 30 MIN.
MAKES 10–15

1 cup (5 oz) uncooked long-grain rice
1/2 cup (3 oz) red gram dal (pigeon peas, toor dal) picked over and rinsed
3 cups (24 fl oz) water
1/2 coconut, grated (approx. 1/2 cup flaked coconut)
6 red chillies (chili peppers)
1/2 teaspoon asafoetida powder
salt to taste
a little water (extra)
oil for shallow-frying

Method

Soak rice and dal in 3 cups (24 fl oz) water for 2 hours. Drain completely. Place in an electric blender or food processor. Add grated coconut, red chillies, asafoetida powder, and salt to taste. Blend ingredients into a fine paste. Add a little extra water only if necessary.

TO PREPARE TAWA: See Ordinary Dosai (p. 84).
TO MAKE DOSAIS: See Dal Dosai (p. 90).
Serve hot with chutney.

If you do not have a tawa or griddle, use a cast-iron frying pan or skillet.

SEMOLINA ADAI
Rava Adai

PREPARATION TIME: 20 MIN. COOKING TIME: 30 MIN.
MAKES 10

1/2 coconut, grated (approx, 1/2 cup flaked coconut)
4 green chillies (chili peppers), finely chopped
a piece of fresh ginger (1 cm/1/2 in long), finely grated
1/2 teaspoon sugar
1 teaspoon cumin seeds
1 tablespoon well-mixed plain yogurt (see p. 136)
salt to taste
water as required
1 3/4 cups (10 oz) semolina, roasted
oil for shallow-frying

Method

In a mixing bowl, combine the grated coconut, finely chopped green chillies, ginger, sugar, cumin seeds, plain yogurt, and salt to taste. Add sufficient water to make a batter and mix thoroughly. Finally, add the semolina, and mix well to make a batter of thick dropping consistency. Add more water if necessary.

TO PREPARE TAWA: See Ordinary Dosai (p. 84).
TO MAKE ADAIS: See Dal Dosai (p. 90).
Serve hot with Coconut Chutney (p. 122).

If you do not have a tawa or griddle, use a cast-iron frying pan or skillet.

OPPOSITE – *Potato Dosai, Spicy Dosai, and Semolina Adai*
PREVIOUS PAGE – *Jaggery Dosai, Dal Dosai, and Green Gram Dosai*

RICE IDLI
Idli

PREPARATION TIME: 16 HRS; COOKING TIME: 15 MIN.
MAKES 25

2 cups (12 oz) parboiled (converted) rice
4 cups (32 fl oz) water
1 cup (6 oz) black gram dal (washed urad dal),
picked over and rinsed
2 cups (16 fl oz) water
a little water (extra)
salt to taste

Method

Soak the parboiled rice and black gram dal separately for 4–5 hours. Soak the rice in 4 cups (32 fl oz) water, and the dal in 2 cups (16 fl oz) water. Completely drain off water from both rice and black gram dal.

Place the soaked dal in an electric blender or food processor. Blend into a very fine batter, adding a little extra water if necessary. Set aside. Now blend or process the soaked rice. This batter should be slightly coarser than that of the dal.

Mix both batters together in a bowl. Add the salt to taste, and set aside to ferment for at least 8 hours. Do not stir the batter before using.*

Using oiled idli moulds, form portions of the rice into idlis (flattened round balls). Steam in the idli moulds in a pressure cooker (without the weight), for 15 minutes. If you do not have either an idli mould or a pressure cooker, form the batter into medium-sized balls with your hands and flatten slightly. Steam in a steamer or on a steamer stand in a saucepan for 15–20 minutes.

Serve hot with Coconut Chutney (p. 122) and Small Onion Sambar (p. 2).

It is very important not to stir the batter before filling the idli moulds. It is the trapped air in this batter that helps to make soft, fluffy idlis.

To make quick and easy idlis, use rice semolina, available in most South Indian provision stores or Indian markets if you cannot find it elsewhere. Soak the rice semolina in place of the parboiled rice. Add the soaked semolina to the ground black gram dal to make the batter. This semolina need not be ground before adding.

To make Idli Uppuma, crumble leftover idlis and season with ½ teaspoon brown mustard seeds, 1 teaspoon black gram dal, a halved red chilli (chili pepper), a chopped green chilli, and a few curry leaves. Dosai Chilli Powder (see p. 139) can also be sprinkled over the cooked idlis.

Leftover idlis can be quartered, and then deep-fried until golden in colour. Cold idlis smeared generously with Dosai Chilli Powder (p. 139) and oil make a delicious snack.

SEMOLINA IDLI
Rava Idli

PREPARATION TIME: 15 MIN. COOKING TIME: 20 MIN.
MAKES 15

3–4 tablespoons ghee
1 cup (5 oz) fine semolina
2 tablespoons raw cashew nuts, halved and chopped
a piece of fresh ginger (2½ cm/1 in long), skinned and grated
2 green chillies (chili peppers), finely chopped
1 small bunch of coriander (Chinese parsley) leaves, finely chopped
½ cup (4 fl oz) plain yogurt (see p. 136)
salt to taste
water as required

FOR TEMPERING

2 teaspoons ghee
1 teaspoon brown mustard seeds
1 teaspoon cumin seeds
a few curry leaves

Method

Heat 2 tablespoons ghee in a heavy frying pan or skillet. Sauté semolina until golden in colour. Remove from the pan. Heat the remaining ghee in the same pan. Sauté the cashew nuts until golden. Set aside.

In a bowl, combine semolina, grated ginger, green chillies, coriander leaves, yogurt, and salt to taste. Add just enough water to make a batter of thick pouring consistency. Mix thoroughly.

TEMPERING: Heat the ghee in a heavy frying pan or skillet. Add mustard seeds, cumin seeds, and a few curry leaves.

When the mustard seeds splutter, add this seasoning to the batter. Mix thoroughly. Add sautéed cashews.

Shape into balls and pressure cook in an idli mould as for Rice Idli (opposite). Once again, if you do not have an idli mould or a pressure cooker, shape the dough into medium-sized balls with your hands, flatten a little, and steam for 15–20 minutes. Test with a skewer or fork; if it comes out clean, the idlis are cooked.

Serve hot with Coconut Chutney (p. 122).

KANCHEEPURAM IDLI

PREPARATION TIME: 24 HRS; COOKING TIME: 20 MIN.
SERVES 4

1½ cups (9 oz) parboiled (converted) rice
1 cup (6 oz) black gram dal (washed urad dal),
picked over and rinsed
5 cups (2 imperial pints) water
a little water (extra)
½ teaspoon asafoetida powder
1 teaspoon crushed black peppercorns
1½ teaspoons ground ginger
1 teaspoon cumin seeds
salt to taste
¼ cup (2 fl oz) sesame or any other oil
¼ cup (2 fl oz) ghee
a few curry leaves
a little oil (extra)

Method

Soak the parboiled rice and black gram dal in 5 cups (2 imperial pints) water for 2 hours. Drain off the water completely.

Place the rice and dal in an electric blender or food processor. Blend ingredients into a coarse batter, adding a little extra water only if necessary. The batter should be of thick pouring consistency.

Place the batter in a large mixing bowl. Add the asafoetida powder, crushed peppercorns, ginger, cumin seeds, and salt to taste. Allow to ferment for 24 hours. The batter should turn sour.

Just before making the idlis, heat the oil and ghee in a heavy frying pan or skillet. Add curry leaves and sauté for 2–3 minutes. Remove from the heat and add to the fermented batter. Mix thoroughly.

Smear oil over the inside of a pan (one that fits inside your pressure cooker or steamer — a shallow cake pan is ideal). Pour batter into the pan. Pressure cook (without the weight) for 20 minutes. If using a steamer, cook for 15–20 minutes. When cooked, cut into triangles.

Serve hot with Coconut Chutney (p. 122).

Do not use the usual perforated idli mould nor shape the mixture into balls to make this spicy idli.

ORDINARY VADAI
Medu Vadai

PREPARATION TIME: 2 HRS 30 MIN. COOKING TIME: 30 MIN.
MAKES 15–20

1 cup (6 oz) black gram dal (washed urad dal),
picked over and rinsed
2 cups (16 fl oz) water
1 teaspoon asafoetida powder
4 green chillies (chili peppers)
salt to taste
a little water (extra)
1 bunch of coriander (Chinese parsley) leaves,
finely chopped
oil for deep-frying

Method

Soak the black gram dal in 2 cups (16 fl oz) water for 2 hours. Drain off water completely. Place dal in an electric blender or food processor. Add the asafoetida powder, green chillies, and salt to taste. Blend into a thick batter, adding a little extra water only if necessary.*

Place the batter in a mixing bowl and add the finely chopped coriander leaves. Mix thoroughly.

TO MAKE VADAIS: Heat oil in a deep-fryer or deep saucepan. Take a ladleful of batter and place it on the palm of one hand. Wet your other hand with water and flatten the batter with this hand. Make a hole in the centre. The vadai will be shaped like a doughnut, and about the same size as one. Slip gently into the oil.

Deep-fry until golden brown and crisp. Drain vadais on brown paper or absorbent kitchen paper. Continue this process until all the batter is used.

Serve hot with chutney.

*This batter should be very thick, otherwise you will not be able to shape it into vadais. If you find it difficult to make the vadais using the method outlined above, try using a sheet of moistened cling wrap or polythene. Place it either on your hand or the kitchen counter. Take a ladleful of batter, flatten it on the sheet, make a hole in the centre, and slip gently into the oil.

Spongy vadais soaked in rasam or sambar are so juicy that they just melt in the mouth.

CABBAGE VADAI

PREPARATION TIME: 2 HRS 30 MIN. COOKING TIME: 30 MIN.
MAKES 15–20

1 cup (6 oz) black gram dal (washed urad dal),
picked over and rinsed
2 cups (16 fl oz) water
1 teaspoon asafoetida powder
4 green chillies (chili peppers)
salt to taste
1/2 cup (approx. 4 oz) cabbage, finely chopped
1 large onion, finely chopped
2 tablespoons shelled green peas (optional)
1 bunch of coriander (Chinese parsley) leaves,
finely chopped
oil for deep-frying

Method

Soak the black gram dal in 2 cups (16 fl oz) water for 2 hours. Drain off water completely. Place dal in an electric blender or food processor. Add the asafoetida powder, green chillies, and salt to taste. Blend into a thick batter.

Place batter in a large mixing bowl. Add the chopped cabbage, onion, peas and coriander leaves. Mix well.

TO MAKE VADAIS: See Ordinary Vadai (opposite).

Serve hot with chutney.

Use chopped spinach instead of cabbage to make crisp and colourful Spinach Vadai (Keerai Vadai).

OPPOSITE – *Ordinary Vadai (bottom left) and Cabbage Vadai (top right)*
PREVIOUS PAGE – *(clockwise from top left) Rice Idli, Kancheepuram Idli, and Semolina Idli*

CURD VADAI
Thair Vadai

PREPARATION TIME: 2 HRS 30 MIN. COOKING TIME: 30 MIN.
MAKES 15–20

1 cup (6 oz) black gram dal (washed urad dal), picked over and rinsed
2 cups (16 fl oz) water
8 green chillies (chili peppers)
salt to taste
3 tablespoons grated fresh coconut or
4 tablespoons flaked coconut
1 teaspoon cumin seeds
4 cups (32 fl oz) plain yogurt (see p. 136)
oil for deep-frying
coriander (Chinese parsley) leaves, chopped (to garnish)

FOR TEMPERING

2 teaspoons oil
1 teaspoon brown mustard seeds
1 teaspoon cumin seeds
1 red chilli (chili pepper), halved
1 teaspoon black gram dal (washed urad dal), picked over and rinsed
½ teaspoon asafoetida powder
a few curry leaves

Method

Soak black gram dal in 2 cups (16 fl oz) water for 2 hours. Drain off water completely. Place in an electric blender or food processor. Add 4 green chillies and salt to taste. Blend into a thick, smooth batter. Set aside.

Now blend or process the coconut, remaining green chillies, and cumin seeds into a fine paste. Add the paste and salt to taste, if needed, to the well-mixed yogurt.

TEMPERING: Heat 2 teaspoons oil in a heavy frying pan or skillet. Add mustard seeds, cumin seeds, halved red chilli, black gram dal, asafoetida powder, and a few curry leaves.

When the mustard seeds splutter, add this mixture to the yogurt and set aside.

TO MAKE VADAIS: Take the prepared batter and cook as for Ordinary Vadai (p. 96).

Arrange vadais in a serving bowl. Pour yogurt mixture over the top. Garnish with coriander leaves and serve.

If the vadais seem hard when cooked, plunge them into warm water. Remove after a minute and squeeze dry.

MASALA VADAI

PREPARATION TIME: 1 HR 30 MIN. COOKING TIME: 30 MIN.
MAKES 15–20

½ cup (3 oz) red gram dal (pigeon peas, toor dal), picked over and rinsed
½ cup (3 oz) black gram dal (washed urad dal), picked over and rinsed
½ cup (3 oz) Bengal gram dal (yellow split peas, chana dal), picked over and rinsed
4½ cups (36 fl oz) water
6 red chillies (chili peppers)
salt to taste
½ cup (4 oz) finely chopped onions
a few curry leaves
1 bunch of coriander (Chinese parsley) leaves, finely chopped
4 green chillies, finely chopped
½ teaspoon asafoetida powder
a piece of fresh ginger (2½ cm/1 in long), finely chopped
oil for deep-frying

Method

Soak the red gram dal, black gram dal and Bengal gram dal in 4½ cups (36 fl oz) water for 1 hour. Drain off excess water completely. Place dals in an electric blender or food processor. Add the 6 red chillies. Blend ingredients into a thick batter.

Place the batter in a large mixing bowl. Add the salt to taste, onions, a few curry leaves, coriander leaves, green chillies, asafoetida powder, and chopped ginger to the batter. Mix thoroughly.

TO MAKE VADAIS: See Ordinary Vadai (p. 96). It is not necessary, however, to make a hole in the centre of the vadais for Masala Vadai.

Serve hot with Coconut Chutney (p. 122).

For a less spicy, yet equally crunchy vadai, leave out the onion and ginger. This dish goes by the quaint name of Amai Vadai.

OPPOSITE – *Curd Vadai (bottom left) and Masala Vadai (top right)*

MYSORE VADAI

PREPARATION TIME: 20 MIN. COOKING TIME: 20 MIN.
MAKES 15

½ cup (4 oz) rice flour
½ cup (5 oz) fine semolina
½ cup (4 oz) plain (all-purpose) flour
¼ cup (2 fl oz) ghee
4–5 green chillies (chili peppers), finely chopped
2 medium-sized onions, finely chopped
1 small bunch of coriander (Chinese parsley) leaves, finely chopped
½ teaspoon asafoetida powder
salt to taste
water as required

Method

Sift rice flour, semolina and plain flour into a large bowl. Add remaining ingredients, minus water, and mix well. Add sufficient water to make a stiff batter. Combine well.
TO MAKE VADAIS: See Ordinary Vadai (p. 96), but do not make a hole in the centre of the vadais.

Serve hot with Mint Chutney (p. 124).

POTATO VADAI
Urulaikizhangu Vadai

PREPARATION TIME: 40 MIN. COOKING TIME: 30 MIN.
MAKES 10–15

350 g (11 oz) potatoes (about 4 medium-sized potatoes)
½ cup (2 oz) Bengal gram flour (besan, chickpea flour)
2 tablespoons rice flour
a piece of fresh ginger (1 cm/½ in), scraped and grated
7–8 green chillies (chili peppers), finely chopped
1 small bunch of coriander (Chinese parsley) leaves, finely chopped
½ teaspoon asafoetida powder
a few curry leaves
salt to taste

FOR TEMPERING

2 teaspoons oil
1 teaspoon brown mustard seeds
a few curry leaves

Method

Boil the potatoes in their jackets. Peel and mash. Place in a large mixing bowl. Add the Bengal gram flour, rice flour, ginger, green chillies, coriander leaves, asafoetida powder, a few curry leaves, and salt to taste.
TEMPERING: Heat 2 teaspoons oil in a heavy frying pan or skillet. Add mustard seeds and a few curry leaves.

When the mustard seeds splutter, add this seasoning to the potato mixture. Mix thoroughly.
TO MAKE VADAIS: See Ordinary Vadai (p. 96), but do not make a hole in the centre of the vadais.

Serve hot with chutney.

Eat these vadais hot. They become soggy when cold.

SAGO VADAI
Javvarisi Vadai

PREPARATION TIME: 40 MIN. COOKING TIME: 20 MIN.
MAKES 10–15

½ cup (3 oz) sago
½ cup (4 fl oz) sour buttermilk*
½ cup (2 oz) Bengal gram flour (besan, chickpea flour)
or rice flour
salt to taste
1 teaspoon red chilli powder
1 teaspoon ghee
2 green chillies (chili peppers), finely chopped
½ teaspoon asafoetida powder
1 small bunch of coriander (Chinese parsley) leaves, finely chopped
oil for deep-frying

Method

Soak the sago in the buttermilk for 30 minutes. Place in a large mixing bowl. Add the Bengal gram flour or rice flour, salt to taste, red chilli powder, ghee, green chillies, asafoetida powder and coriander. Combine ingredients thoroughly to make a thick batter. Add water if necessary.
TO MAKE VADAIS: See Ordinary Vadai (p. 96), but do not make a hole in the centre of the vadais.

Serve hot with chutney.

*If you do not have any sour buttermilk, add 1 teaspoon malt vinegar to normal buttermilk. Proceed as instructed.

OPPOSITE – *Mysore Vadai, Potato Vadai, and Sago Vadai*

POTATO BONDA
Urulaikizhangu Bonda

PREPARATION TIME: 45 MIN. COOKING TIME: 30 MIN.
MAKES 10–15

4 large potatoes
4 green chillies (chili peppers), finely chopped
a piece of fresh ginger (2½ cm/1 in), finely chopped
2 large onions, finely chopped
salt to taste
½ teaspoon ground turmeric
1 bunch of coriander (Chinese parsley) leaves,
finely chopped
oil for deep-frying

FOR TEMPERING

3 teaspoons ghee
1 teaspoon brown mustard seeds
1 teaspoon black gram dal (washed urad dal),
picked over and rinsed
1 red chilli (chili pepper), halved
a few curry leaves

BATTER

2 cups (8 oz) Bengal gram flour (besan, chickpea flour)
2 teaspoons red chilli powder
¼ teaspoon asafoetida powder
salt to taste
water as required

Method

Boil the potatoes in their jackets. Peel, mash and set aside.
TEMPERING: Heat 3 teaspoons ghee in a heavy saucepan. Add the mustard seeds, black gram dal, halved red chilli, and a few curry leaves.

When the mustard seeds splutter, add finely chopped green chillies, ginger and onions. Sauté for 2–3 minutes.

Add mashed potatoes, salt to taste, ground turmeric, and chopped coriander leaves. Cook for 2–3 minutes until thoroughly blended. Remove from heat and cool.

Shape the potato mixture into lemon-sized balls. Set aside.
TO MAKE BATTER: In a large mixing bowl, combine the Bengal gram flour, red chilli powder, asafoetida powder, and salt to taste. Add enough water to make a smooth batter of dropping consistency.

Heat oil for deep-frying. Dip each potato ball into the batter and fry until golden brown in colour.

Serve hot with chutney.

For a tangy taste, squeeze lime juice into the potato mixture.

For variety, put a little green chutney in the centre of the potato balls. Dip into the batter and fry as usual.

VEGETABLE BONDA

PREPARATION TIME: 1 HR 30 MIN. COOKING TIME: 30 MIN.
MAKES 15–20

1 cup (6 oz) Bengal gram dal (yellow split peas,
chana dal), picked over and rinsed
2 cups (16 fl oz) water
4 red chillies (chili peppers)
1 teaspoon asafoetida powder
salt to taste
½ cup (approx. 4 oz) cauliflower, cut into small florets
¼ cup (approx. 1 oz) green peas
1 onion, finely chopped
a few curry leaves
oil for frying

Method

Soak the Bengal gram dal in 2 cups (16 fl oz) water for 1 hour. Drain off excess water and place the dal in an electric blender or food processor. Add the red chillies, asafoetida powder, and salt to taste. Blend ingredients into a smooth batter.

Add the cauliflower, green peas, finely chopped onion, and a few curry leaves to the batter. Mix thoroughly.

Heat oil in a heavy frying pan or skillet. Shape the batter into small balls and fry until golden.

Drain the cooked bondas on a sheet of brown paper or absorbent kitchen paper.

Serve hot with chutney.

The batter should be thick so that it can be shaped easily into balls and slipped into the oil.

OPPOSITE – *(clockwise from bottom left) Mysore Bonda, Vegetable Bonda, and Potato Bonda*

Mysore Bonda

PREPARATION TIME: 2 HRS 30 MIN. COOKING TIME: 30 MIN.
MAKES 15–20

1 cup (6 oz) black gram dal (washed urad dal), picked over and rinsed
2 cups (16 fl oz) water
salt to taste
1 teaspoon whole black peppercorns
1/4 cup chopped coconut pieces
or 5 1/2 tablespoons flaked coconut
1/2 teaspoon asafoetida powder
a few curry leaves
oil for frying

Method

Soak the black gram dal in 2 cups (16 fl oz) water for 2 hours. Drain off excess water completely. Place dal in an electric blender or food processor. Blend into a smooth batter. Add the salt to taste, black peppercorns, coconut, asafoetida powder, and a few curry leaves. Mix thoroughly.

Heat oil in a heavy frying pan or skillet. Shape the batter into lemon-sized balls, and drop gently into the oil. Fry until golden in colour.

Drain the cooked bondas on a sheet of brown paper or absorbent kitchen paper.

Serve hot with Coconut Chutney (p. 122).

VEGETABLE BAJJI

**PREPARATION TIME: 20 MIN. COOKING TIME: 20 MIN.
MAKES 15–20**

Any of the following vegetables* can be used to make bajji:
1 raw green plantain, peeled and cut into thin slices
1 potato, peeled and sliced
1 onion, peeled and sliced
1 choko (chayote), peeled and sliced
1 ridge gourd, peeled and sliced
cauliflower, cut into florets
oil for deep-frying

BATTER

1 cup (4 oz) Bengal gram flour (besan, chickpea flour)
1 teaspoon red chilli powder
1/2 teaspoon ground coriander
1/2 teaspoon asafoetida powder
1 1/2 tablespoons rice flour
salt to taste
1/2 teaspoon cumin seeds
1 teaspoon ghee
water as required

Method

TO MAKE BATTER: Sift the Bengal gram flour, red chilli powder, ground coriander, asafoetida powder, rice flour, and salt to taste into a large mixing bowl. Add the cumin seeds and ghee. Combine ingredients well. Add sufficient water to make a thick batter of pouring consistency, and beat until smooth.

Peel and prepare the vegetables as necessary. Wash the vegetable slices or florets and pat dry.

Heat oil in a heavy frying pan or skillet. Dip the vegetable slices into the batter, and deep-fry until golden in colour.

Drain the bajjis on a sheet of brown paper or absorbent kitchen paper.

Serve hot with chutney or tomato ketchup.

* If you combine a couple of vegetables, use 1 cup peeled and sliced vegetables to 1 1/3 cups of the batter.

Adding 2 tablespoons leftover sour dosai batter (see p. 84) to the bajji batter makes very crisp, tangy bajjis.

SUNDAL

**PREPARATION TIME: 10 HRS; COOKING TIME: 10 MIN.
SERVES 4**

1 cup (6 oz) chickpeas (garbanzo beans, kabli chana)
3 cups (24 fl oz) water
1/2 green mango, peeled and finely chopped
1 green chilli (chili pepper), finely chopped
2 tablespoons grated fresh coconut
or 2 1/2 tablespoons flaked coconut
salt to taste
juice of 1 lemon

FOR TEMPERING

2 teaspoons oil
1 teaspoon brown mustard seeds
1 teaspoon black gram dal (washed urad dal),
picked over and rinsed
1 red chilli (chili pepper), halved
1/2 teaspoon asafoetida powder

Method

Soak the chickpeas in a cool place for 7–8 hours. Drain off water and place chickpeas in a saucepan. Cover with at least 3 cups (24 fl oz) of water and bring to the boil. When boiling, cover pan with a lid. Simmer gently for 30–45 minutes until soft. When cooked, drain chickpeas and set aside.

TEMPERING:

Heat 2 teaspoons oil in a heavy saucepan. Add the mustard seeds, black gram dal, halved red chilli, and asafoetida powder.

When the mustard seeds splutter, add boiled chickpeas.

Now add the mango, green chilli, coconut, and salt to taste. Mix thoroughly. Remove from heat and add the lemon juice.

Serve hot or cold.

Sundal is delicious served either as a snack or a salad.

Equally mouth-watering savoury sundals can be made with boiled peanuts, split peas (matar dal) or any other lentil or pulse.

OPPOSITE – *Sundal (bottom left), Onion Pakoras (near right), and Vegetable Bajji (top right)*
FOLLOWING PAGE – *Vegetable Rava Uppuma (top), Beaten Rice Uppuma (bottom right), and Yam Chips (bottom left)*

ONION PAKORA
Vengaya Pakora

PREPARATION TIME: 25 MIN. COOKING TIME: 20 MIN.
MAKES 15–20

2 teaspoons ghee
a pinch of bicarbonate of soda (baking soda)
1 cup (4 oz) Bengal gram flour (besan, chickpea flour)
½ cup (2 oz) rice flour
2 tablespoons ghee
3 onions, finely chopped
1 potato, finely chopped (optional)
a piece of fresh ginger (2½ cm/ 1in),
scraped and finely chopped
4 green chillies (chili peppers), finely chopped

1 teaspoon red chilli powder
1 bunch of coriander (Chinese parsley)
leaves, finely chopped
salt to taste
water as required
oil for deep-frying

Method

Place 2 teaspoons ghee and bicarbonate of soda in a mixing bowl. Rub together until frothy. Add the remaining ingredients and combine well, using sufficient water to make a thick batter.

Heat oil in a heavy frying pan or skillet. Drop spoonfuls of batter into the oil. Fry the pakoras until golden in colour. When cooked, drain the excess oil on a sheet of brown paper or absorbent kitchen paper.

Serve hot with chutney or tomato ketchup.

YAM CHIPS
Chenaikizhangu Varuval

PREPARATION TIME: 45 MIN. COOKING TIME: 30 MIN.
SERVES 4

2 teaspoons ground turmeric
4 cups (32 fl oz) water
1 kg (2 lbs) yam*
oil for deep-frying
2 teaspoons chilli powder
1 teaspoon asafoetida powder
salt to taste

Method

Add ground turmeric to 4 cups (32 fl oz) water and set aside. Peel the yam and slice thinly. Immerse in the turmeric solution for 30 minutes. Drain, pat dry with a clean towel, and spread the yam chips on a thin cloth.

Heat oil in a heavy pan and deep-fry the chips. Mix the chilli powder, asafoetida powder, and salt to taste together. Sprinkle over the cooked yam chips.

Serve immediately or store in an airtight container.

*You can also make crispy, crunchy chips from sweet potatoes or kumara, potatoes, raw green plantains, and tapioca. Simply follow the instructions given above.

BEATEN RICE UPPUMA
Aval Uppuma

PREPARATION TIME: 20 MIN. COOKING TIME: 20 MIN.
SERVES 4

1¹/₂ cups (8 oz) beaten rice*
2 onions, finely chopped
4 green chillies (chili peppers), finely chopped
2 potatoes, peeled and finely chopped
¹/₂ teaspoon ground turmeric
salt to taste
water as required
3 tablespoons grated fresh coconut or
4 tablespoons flaked coconut
juice of 1 lemon (optional)
1 small bunch of coriander (Chinese parsley)
leaves (to garnish)

FOR TEMPERING
2 tablespoons oil
1 teaspoon brown mustard seeds
1 teaspoon cumin seeds
¹/₄ teaspoon asafoetida powder
1 red chilli (chili pepper), halved
a few curry leaves

Method

Wash the beaten rice thoroughly. Drain and set aside.

TEMPERING: Heat 2 tablespoons oil in a heavy saucepan. Add mustard seeds, cumin seeds, asafoetida powder, halved red chilli, and a few curry leaves.

When the mustard seeds splutter, add onions and green chillies. Sauté for 2–3 minutes. Add potatoes, ground turmeric, and salt to taste. Barely cover with water and cook until the potato is tender. Add the washed beaten rice. Stir well. Cook until water has been absorbed and mixture is completely dry. Add coconut. Remove from heat. Add lemon juice if desired.

Garnish with coriander and serve hot.

*Beaten rice is precisely what the name suggests — rice that has been beaten flat. It should be available from Indian markets or Asian food stores.

VEGETABLE RAVA UPPUMA

PREPARATION TIME: 15 MIN. COOKING TIME: 20 MIN.
SERVES 4

1 cup (6 oz) semolina
2 onions, finely chopped
a piece of fresh ginger (1 cm/¹/₂ in),
scraped and finely chopped
2–3 green chillies (chili peppers), finely chopped
1 potato, finely chopped
1 sweet pepper (capsicum), finely chopped
1 small carrot, finely chopped
3 green or string beans, finely chopped
¹/₄ cup (approx. 1 oz) shelled green peas (optional)
¹/₂ teaspoon ground turmeric
salt to taste
3 cups (24 fl oz) water
juice of 1 lemon
1 small bunch of coriander (Chinese parsley)
leaves, finely chopped (to garnish)

FOR TEMPERING

3 tablespoons ghee or oil
1 teaspoon brown mustard seeds
1 teaspoon cumin seeds
1 teaspoon black gram dal (washed urad dal),
picked over and rinsed
1 teaspoon Bengal gram dal (yellow split peas,
chana dal), picked over and rinsed
½ teaspoon asafoetida powder
1 red chilli (chili pepper), halved
a few curry leaves

Method

Dry-roast semolina lightly in a heavy saucepan. Set aside.

TEMPERING: Heat 3 tablespoons ghee in a heavy saucepan. Add mustard seeds, cumin seeds, black gram dal, Bengal gram dal, asafoetida powder, halved red chilli, and a few curry leaves.

When the mustard seeds splutter, add onions, ginger, and green chillies. Sauté for 2–3 minutes. Now add the potatoes, pepper, carrot, beans, peas, ground turmeric, and salt to taste. Sauté for 1 minute. Add 3 cups (24 fl oz) water. Cover pan and simmer over a low heat until the vegetables are tender.

Gradually add semolina. Stir constantly to prevent lumps. Cook until all the water has been absorbed. Remove from heat.

Add lemon juice. Garnish with coriander. Serve hot.

Semolina comes in various grades of coarseness. The fine-grained sort will cook in very little water. Conversely, always cook coarse-grained semolina with more water than stated in the recipe above. If the semolina is still uncooked after the water has been absorbed, add a little more water to the pan and continue cooking as before.

DESSERTS & SWEET TREATS

These desserts and sweets (candies) can be served at any time of the day — to round off a meal, as a morning or afternoon snack, or when unexpected, or even expected, guests call. Most of the burfis and laddus can be stored for several days in airtight containers.

~

On extra special occasions, payasams are considered indispensable in South Indian homes. More often than not, jaggery is used as the sweetening agent. Earthy, subtly flavoured and less sweet than refined sugar, jaggery gives payasams their unusual and distinctive taste.

MILK PAYASAM
Paal Payasam

PREPARATION TIME: 10 MIN. COOKING TIME: 1 HR 30 MIN.
SERVES 4

12 cups (3 litres, 5 imperial pints) milk
1/4 cup (1 1/2 oz) long-grained rice
1/2 cup (4 oz) sugar
6–8 whole cardamoms, crushed
1 teaspoon saffron
1/2 cup (4 fl oz) warm milk (extra)

Method

Place the milk and rice in a heavy saucepan and bring to the boil, stirring continuously. Keep stirring and simmer until the milk reduces to half its original quantity.

Now add the sugar and crushed cardamoms.

Dissolve the saffron in 1/2 cup (4 fl oz) warm milk and add to the payasam. Stir thoroughly.

Serve hot or chilled.

VERMICELLI PAYASAM
Semiya Payasam

PREPARATION TIME: 10 MIN. COOKING TIME: 40 MIN.
SERVES 6

8 cups (2 litres, 3 1/4 imperial pints) milk
1/4 cup (2 oz) ghee
2 tablespoons raw cashew nuts, halved
1 tablespoon raisins
1 cup (6 oz) vermicelli, broken into 4 cm (1 1/2 in) lengths
1/2 cup (4 oz) sugar
4 whole cardamoms, crushed
1/2 teaspoon saffron

Method

Place the milk in a heavy saucepan and, stirring constantly, bring to the boil. Keep stirring and simmer until the milk is reduced to three-quarters its original quantity. Do not remove from heat.

In the meantime, heat the ghee in a heavy frying pan or skillet. Sauté the cashew nuts and raisins for 2–3 minutes. Remove and set aside.

In the same ghee, sauté the vermicelli until it turns reddish in colour. Add to the reduced milk, which should still be boiling. Continue cooking until the vermicelli is well done.

Lastly, add the sugar, crushed cardamoms, and saffron. Stir thoroughly.

Garnish with the sautéed cashew nuts and raisins. Serve hot or chilled.

CARROT & CASHEW PAYASAM
Carrot Mundriparupu Payasam

PREPARATION TIME: 35 MIN. COOKING TIME: 40 MIN.
SERVES 4

1/2 cup (3 oz) raw cashew nuts
1 cup (8 fl oz) warm milk
6 cups (1 1/2 litres, 2 1/2 imperial pints) milk (extra)
2 tablespoons ghee
1 1/2 cups (10 oz) grated carrot
1/2 cup (4 oz) sugar
6 whole cardamoms, crushed

Method

Soak the cashew nuts in 1 cup (8 fl oz) warm milk for 30 minutes.

Place the extra 6 cups (1 1/2 litres, 2 1/2 imperial pints) milk in a heavy saucepan. Bring to the boil, stirring continuously. Keep stirring and simmer until the milk reduces to half its original quantity.

In the meantime, heat 2 tablespoons ghee in a heavy frying pan or skillet. Add the grated carrot and sauté for 5 minutes.

Place sautéed carrot and soaked cashew nuts in an electric blender or food processor. Blend ingredients to a coarse paste. Add this paste to the boiling milk. Stir well.

Now add the sugar and simmer until thoroughly blended. Lastly, add the crushed cardamoms.

Serve chilled.

OPPOSITE – *Carrot & Cashew Payasam (top), Milk Payasam (middle left), and Vermicelli Payasam (bottom)*

ALMOND PAYASAM
Badam Payasam

PREPARATION TIME: 2 HRS 20 MIN. COOKING TIME: 30 MIN.
SERVES 6

1 cup (5 oz) whole almonds
hot water
8 cups (2 litres, 3¼ imperial pints) milk
½ cup (4 oz) sugar
4 whole cardamoms, crushed
1 teaspoon ground nutmeg
1 teaspoon saffron

Method

Soak the almonds in a bowl of hot water for 2 hours. Peel off skins and discard. Place almonds in an electric blender or food processor. Blend to a fine paste and set aside.

Place the milk in a heavy saucepan. Bring to the boil, stirring constantly. Keep stirring and simmer until the milk is reduced to three-quarters its original quantity.

Add the almond paste, sugar, crushed cardamoms, ground nutmeg, and saffron. Simmer on a low heat for 5 minutes.

Serve chilled.

CREAMY MILK PUDDING
Basundi

PREPARATION TIME: 10 MIN. COOKING TIME: 1 HR 30 MIN.
SERVES 4–6

12 cups (3 litres, 5 imperial pints) milk
½ cup (4 oz) sugar
6–8 whole cardamoms, crushed
1 teaspoon saffron
¼ cup (2 fl oz) hot milk (extra)
2 tablespoons chopped pistachios (to garnish)

Method

Place the milk in a heavy saucepan and bring to the boil, stirring constantly. Keep stirring and simmer until the milk reduces to one-third its original quantity.

Add the sugar and simmer for 5 more minutes. Now add the crushed cardamoms. Dissolve the saffron in ¼ cup (2 fl oz) hot milk, and add to the milk pudding. Stir thoroughly.

Garnish with the chopped pistachios. Serve chilled.

SWEET PONGAL
Chakra Pongal

PREPARATION TIME: 20 MIN. COOKING TIME: 45 MIN.
SERVES 4

½ cup (3 oz) green gram dal (split mung beans,
moong dal), picked over and rinsed
1 cup (5 oz) uncooked long-grain rice
2½ cups (20 fl oz) water
1 cup (8 fl oz) milk
3 cups (21 oz) powdered jaggery
¾ cup (6 fl oz) water (extra)
4 tablespoons ghee
2 tablespoons raw cashew nuts
2 tablespoons raisins
5 whole cardamoms, crushed
2 cloves, crushed
a small piece nutmeg, grated
a pinch of saffron

Method

Wash the green gram dal well. Dry-roast in a heavy saucepan for 2–3 minutes. Remove from the heat.

Add the rice, 2½ cups (20 fl oz) water and 1 cup (8 fl oz) milk to the same pan and return to the heat. Cook until rice is soft. Set aside.

In a heavy saucepan, dissolve the jaggery in the extra water. Cook on a low heat until the jaggery melts. Strain the jaggery to remove any impurities. Return the syrup to the heat and stir until it becomes slightly sticky. Add the cooked rice and dal.

Heat 4 tablespoons ghee in a heavy frying pan or skillet. Sauté cashew nuts and raisins for 2–3 minutes. Add the sautéed cashews and raisins to the pongal.

Lastly, add the crushed cardamoms, cloves, nutmeg, and saffron.* Stir thoroughly.

Serve hot.

*If you do not have a mortar and pestle, these spices can be easily ground to a powder in an electric blender or food processor.

OPPOSITE – (clockwise from top left) Semolina Pudding, Sweet Pongal, Creamy Milk Pudding, and Almond Payasam

SEMOLINA PUDDING
Rava Kesari

PREPARATION TIME: 10 MIN. COOKING TIME: 20 MIN
SERVES 4

¼ cup (2 oz) ghee
1 cup (6 oz) semolina
1½ cups (12 fl oz) boiling water
1¼ cups (10 oz) sugar
6 whole cardamoms, crushed
a few saffron threads
2 tablespoons ghee
approx. 20 raw cashew nuts, halved
1 tablespoon raisins

Method

Heat ¼ cup (2 oz) ghee in a heavy saucepan. Add the semolina and sauté until almost golden in colour.

In the meantime, boil some water, and add 1½ cups (12 fl oz) to the semolina when ready. Allow to cook for 2–3 minutes.

Add the sugar, crushed cardamoms, and saffron. Continue cooking until everything is thoroughly blended.

In another pan, heat the remaining 2 tablespoons ghee. Sauté the halved cashew nuts and raisins for 2–3 minutes. Add to the pudding.

Serve hot.

Semolina Pudding can be served straight onto individual plates. You can also transfer the pudding onto a greased plate. Cut it neatly into diamonds and garnish with fried cashew nuts and raisins. It may be served hot or cold.

Jaggery Pancake
Polli

PREPARATION TIME: 20 MIN. COOKING TIME: 2 HRS
MAKES 20–25

2¼ cups (9 oz) plain (all-purpose) flour
½ teaspoon salt
½ teaspoon ground turmeric
¾ cup (6 fl oz) sesame oil
water as required
a few plantain or banana leaves*
a little sesame oil (extra)

FILLING

1½ cups (9 oz) Bengal gram dal (yellow split peas,
chana dal), picked over and rinsed
½ cup (3 oz) red gram dal (pigeon peas, toor dal),
picked over and rinsed
8 cups (2 litres, 3¼ imperial pints)
1 coconut, grated (approx. 1 cup flaked coconut)
1½ kg (3 lbs) jaggery, powdered
4–6 whole cardamoms, powdered

Method

FILLING: Wash Bengal gram dal and red gram dal well. Drain and place dals in a heavy saucepan. Cover with 8 cups (3¼ imperial pints) water and bring to the boil. When boiling, cover pan with a lid, leaving slightly ajar. Lower heat, and simmer the dal gently for 1½ hours. Stir several times during the last 30 minutes of cooking. Set dal aside without draining.

In a heavy saucepan, dry-roast the grated coconut for 2–3 minutes. Add the powdered jaggery and simmer on a low heat until the jaggery completely melts.

Add the cooked dals and continue to simmer until the mixture blends and thickens. Set aside to cool.

Place the cooled filling in an electric blender or food processor. Add the powdered cardamom. Blend ingredients into a fine paste.

TO MAKE DOUGH: Sift the flour, salt and ground turmeric into a large mixing bowl. Make a well in the centre and add ¼ cup (2 fl oz) sesame oil and sufficient water to make a kneadable dough (it should resemble a chapatti or unleavened bread dough). Knead slightly and form into a ball. Pour the remaining sesame oil over the dough. Set aside the dough for 20 minutes, then mix.

Brush the plantain or banana leaves with sesame oil. Take a small ball of the dough and place it on an oiled leaf. Flatten the

dough with your hand, until it resembles a chapatti. Take a small lump of the filling and place it in the centre of the flattened dough. Fold the dough over the filling. Once again, flatten the pancake with your hand (as you would a stuffed potato paratha).**

Heat a tawa or griddle. Add very little sesame oil and cook both sides until done, as you would an ordinary pancake.

Serve hot or cold with ghee.

* If no plantain or banana leaves are available, you can use an oiled polythene sheet.

** Once you have shaped the pancake, you can put aside the banana or plantain leaf for further use. If it tears, however, discard.

These scrumptious pollis can be kept fresh for a couple of days if stored in an airtight container. They can also be stored in the refrigerator.

Semolina Laddu
Rava Laddu

PREPARATION TIME: 20 MIN. COOKING TIME: 10 MIN.
MAKES 15

½ cup (4 oz) ghee
1½ cups (8 oz) semolina
1½ cups (12 oz) sugar
4–5 whole cardamoms, peeled and powdered
2 tablespoons cashew nuts, broken into small pieces
2 tablespoons raisins

Method

Heat 2 tablespoons of the ghee in a heavy saucepan. Add the semolina and roast until light golden in colour.

Place the roasted semolina, sugar and cardamom in an electric blender or food processor. Blend ingredients into a fine powder.

Heat the remaining ghee in a heavy saucepan. Sauté the cashew nuts and raisins for 2–3 minutes. Add to the semolina/sugar mixture and combine thoroughly.

Shape into tight laddus or small balls. The laddus can be stored in an airtight container for a few days.

These laddus break easily, so be sure to store them very carefully.

OPPOSITE – Sesame Toffee (top left), Semolina Laddu (top right), and Jaggery Pancake (bottom left)

SESAME TOFFEE
Ellu Urundai

**PREPARATION TIME: 20 MIN. COOKING TIME: 30 MIN.
MAKES 20–25**

4 cups (1 lb) white sesame seeds
½ cup (4 fl oz) water
1½ cups (8 oz) powdered jaggery
¼ coconut, cut into very small pieces

Method

In a heavy saucepan, dry-roast the sesame seeds until light brown in colour. Set aside

Prepare syrup by adding ½ cup (4 fl oz) water to a heavy saucepan. Add the powdered jaggery and slowly bring to the boil. Now add the chopped coconut pieces. Simmer on a low heat until the syrup becomes thick and sticky.

Add the roasted sesame seeds. Mix thoroughly.

Turn off the heat and quickly shape the mixture into small balls with your fingers.

Store in an airtight container.

MILK DELIGHT
Paal Mithai

PREPARATION TIME: 5 MIN. COOKING TIME: 1 HOUR
MAKES 20

3 cups (24 fl oz) milk
2 cups (1 lb) sugar
1/2 cup (4 oz) ghee
1/4 cup (1 1/2 oz) semolina
2 tablespoons ghee (extra)

Method

Place the milk, sugar, ghee and semolina in a heavy saucepan. Cook over a low heat. Keep stirring constantly, until the mixture reaches a thick, sticky consistency.

In the meantime, prepare a serving plate by rubbing the extra ghee evenly on all sides.

Pour the thick mixture onto the greased plate. While still hot, cut into squares.

Allow to cool and serve.

PEANUT TOFFEE
Verkadalai Burfi

PREPARATION TIME: 10 MIN. COOKING TIME: 20 MIN.
MAKES 15 PIECES

3/4 cup (6 oz) sugar
butter or ghee (for greasing)
1 cup (5 oz) peanuts, partly broken and roasted

Method

Melt the sugar in a heavy saucepan.

In the meantime, grease a plate, preferably a flat one, with the butter or ghee.

As soon as the sugar melts to one-string or thread consistency, i.e. 110°–112°C (230°–234°F), add the peanuts. Mix quickly and pour onto the greased plate.

Roll out flat with a greased rolling pin. Do this as quickly as possible before the mixture cools.

Cut into squares while still hot. Allow to cool and serve. (Alternatively, you can break the toffee into chunks with a knife when it has set.)

LADDU
Kunjaladu

PREPARATION TIME: 20 MIN. COOKING TIME: 1 HOUR
MAKES 15–20

1 1/2 cups (12 fl oz) water
3 cups (24 oz) sugar
a few saffron threads
4 whole cardamoms, powdered
2 1/2 cups (10 oz) Bengal gram flour
(besan, chickpea flour)
water as required
oil for deep-frying
10 cashew nuts, chopped into small pieces
10 raisins
2 tablespoons ghee
2 tablespoons diamond-shaped rock candy (optional)

Method

In a heavy saucepan, add 1 1/2 cups (12 fl oz) water to the sugar and bring to the boil. Remove the scum from the surface. Boil mixture until it is a syrup of one-string or thread consistency, i.e. 110°–112°C (230°–234°F).

Remove from the heat and add the saffron and powdered cardamoms. Set aside.

Sift the Bengal gram flour into a bowl. Add enough water to make a thick batter of dropping consistency.

Heat oil in a pan. Drop a ladleful of the batter through a slotted spoon with pea-sized holes. Fry until uniformly golden and crisp. Continue until all the batter has been used. Add these balls or *boondis*, as they are known, to the sugar syrup.

Sauté the cashew nuts and raisins in 2 tablespoons ghee, and add to the laddu mixture. Now add the rock candy, if desired. Mix thoroughly and allow to cool.

Shape laddus into small balls.

OPPOSITE – *Peanut Toffee (top left), Laddu (bottom right), and Milk Delight (bottom left)*

GRAM FLOUR BURFI
Mysore Pak

PREPARATION TIME: 5 MIN. COOKING TIME: 40 MIN
MAKES 15–20

2 tablespoons ghee
2 cups (1 lb) ghee (extra)
1 cup (4 oz) Bengal gram flour (besan, chickpea flour), sifted
2 cups (1 lb) sugar
water to cover the sugar

Method

Grease a plate evenly with 2 tablespoons ghee. Set aside.

Heat 1 cup (8 oz) of the extra ghee in a heavy saucepan. Add the sifted Bengal gram flour. Stir thoroughly and set aside.

Now heat the sugar on a low heat, adding just enough water to cover the sugar, and make a syrup of one-string or thread consistency, i.e. 110°–112°C (230°–234°F). Strain the syrup to remove any scum.

Meanwhile, heat the remaining 1 cup (8 oz) ghee.

Add the Bengal gram flour/ghee mixture to the sugar syrup. Keep stirring on a low heat and remove any lumps. Gradually add the remaining heated ghee. Keep stirring until the ghee separates and floats on top.

When the mixture froths up, pour quickly onto the greased plate. Shake the plate gently to spread the burfi.

When the burfi has partly cooled, cut into pieces with a sharp, greased knife.

Store in an airtight container.

COCONUT BURFI
Thengai Burfi

PREPARATION TIME: 15 MIN. COOKING TIME: 20 MIN.
MAKES 15

2 teaspoons ghee
1 cup (8 oz) sugar
1 cup (8 fl oz) water
1 cup (3 oz) finely grated fresh or dessicated coconut
6 whole cardamoms, crushed
¼ cup (2 oz) cashew nuts, chopped

Method

Grease a plate with the ghee and set aside.

Heat the sugar and water on a low heat to make a thick syrup.*

Remove any scum from the syrup. Add the finely grated coconut and crushed cardamoms. Mix thoroughly.

Turn off the heat while the mixture is still a thick pouring consistency. Add the chopped cashew nuts. Mix thoroughly.

Pour the coconut mixture onto the greased plate and quickly spread with a spatula.

After a few minutes, cut into diamond-shaped pieces with a sharp knife.

Store in an airtight container.

Make sure the syrup is very thick before you add the coconut and cardamom, otherwise the burfi will not set.

OPPOSITE – *Coconut Burfi (top) and Gram Flour Burfi (bottom)*

CHUTNEYS & PICKLES

There are chutneys and there are chutneys. The recipes in this chapter definitely fall into the category of something special. Almost all South Indian snacks are served with chutney on the side. Choose your favourite flavour or offer several different chutneys for variety.

Though classified as chutneys, 'thuvaiyals' are eaten with rice. Simply mix them with plain hot rice and a few drops of melted ghee. Easy and quick to prepare, they make delicious light meals. Serve thuvaiyals in the evening as they do in most South Indian homes, since they are easily digestible. If you have made a rich spicy sambar or rasam, eating a light thuvaiyal as your other course offers the perfect balance.

In any South Indian home, you will always find neatly arranged jars of pickles. It goes without saying that they are hot and spicy, but they can also be aromatic and add bite to a meal. Perk up any ordinary dish with a pickle. Most pickles are easy to make and some last for months.

COCONUT CHUTNEY 1

Thengai Chutney 1

**PREPARATION TIME: 20 MIN. COOKING TIME: 3 MIN.
SERVES 4**

*6 tablespoons grated fresh coconut or
8 tablespoons flaked coconut
4 tablespoons fried gram dal, picked over and rinsed*
6 green chillies (chili peppers)
1 small bunch of coriander (Chinese parsley) leaves
a piece of fresh ginger (1 cm/½ in long), finely shredded
a marble-sized piece of tamarind pulp
salt to taste
a little water*

FOR TEMPERING

*2 teaspoons oil
1 teaspoon brown mustard seeds
1 teaspoon cumin seeds
1 teaspoon black gram dal (washed urad dal),
picked over and rinsed
1 red chilli (chili pepper), halved
½ teaspoon asafoetida powder
a few curry leaves*

Method

Place the coconut, fried gram dal, green chillies, coriander leaves, shredded ginger, tamarind pulp, and salt to taste in an electric blender or food processor. Blend ingredients, adding just enough water to make a fine paste.

TEMPERING: Heat 2 teaspoons oil in a heavy frying pan or skillet. Add the mustard seeds, cumin seeds, black gram dal, halved red chilli, asafoetida powder, and a few curry leaves.

When the mustard seeds splutter, add this mixture to the chutney paste. Mix thoroughly.

Serve with dosais, idlis and vadais.

*Fried gram dal is roasted and puffed Bengal gram dal. If you are unable to find this ingredient at Indian markets or Asian food stores, dry-roasted Bengal gram dal (yellow split peas, chana dal) may be used as a substitute.

Vary the consistency of the chutney according to your taste and requirements. However, when making Masala Dosai, always make sure that the chutney is thick. Otherwise it will be difficult to spread over the dosai.

COCONUT CHUTNEY 2

Thengai Chutney 2

**PREPARATION TIME: 20 MIN. COOKING TIME: 3 MIN.
SERVES 4**

*2 teaspoons oil
3 tablespoons Bengal gram dal (yellow split peas,
chana dal), picked over and rinsed
4–5 red chillies (chili peppers)
½ teaspoon asafoetida powder
6 tablespoons grated fresh coconut or
8 tablespoons flaked coconut
salt to taste
a little water
coriander (Chinese parsley) leaves,
finely chopped (to garnish)*

FOR TEMPERING

*2 teaspoons oil
1 teaspoon brown mustard seeds
1 teaspoon cumin seeds
1 teaspoon black gram dal (washed urad dal),
picked over and rinsed
1 red chilli (chili pepper), halved
a few curry leaves*

Method

Heat 2 teaspoons oil in a heavy frying pan or skillet. Add the Bengal gram dal, red chillies, and asafoetida powder. Sauté for 2–3 minutes, or until the dal turns golden.

Place this mixture in an electric blender or food processor. Add the grated coconut and salt to taste. Blend ingredients to a fine paste, adding very little water — just enough to make the paste smooth. Set aside.

TEMPERING: Heat 2 teaspoons oil in a heavy frying pan or skillet. Add mustard seeds, cumin seeds, black gram dal, halved red chilli, and a few curry leaves.

When the mustard seeds splutter, add this mixture to the chutney paste. Mix thoroughly.

Garnish with the chopped coriander leaves and serve with dosais, idlis or vadais.

OPPOSITE – *Coconut Chutneys 1 and 2*

BROWN COCONUT CHUTNEY

Thengai Thuvaiyal

PREPARATION TIME: 20 MIN. COOKING TIME: 3 MIN.
SERVES 4

1 tablespoon oil
3–4 teaspoons Bengal gram dal (yellow split peas,
chana dal), picked over and rinsed
1 tablespoon black gram dal (washed urad dal),
picked over and rinsed
2 red chillies (chili peppers)
3 green chillies (chili peppers)
1/2 teaspoon asafoetida powder
2 teaspoons brown mustard seeds
6 tablespoons grated fresh coconut or
8 tablespoons flaked coconut
a marble-sized piece of tamarind pulp
1 small bunch of coriander (Chinese parsley) leaves
salt to taste

Method

Heat 1 tablespoon oil in a heavy frying pan or skillet. Sauté the Bengal gram dal, black gram dal, red chillies, green chillies, asafoetida powder, and mustard seeds until the dals turn golden.

Place this mixture in an electric blender or food processor. Add the grated coconut, tamarind pulp, coriander leaves, and salt to taste. Blend ingredients, adding sufficient water to make a fine paste.

Serve with hot rice and ghee, or dosais.

MINT CHUTNEY

Pudina Thuvaiyal

PREPARATION TIME: 20 MIN. COOKING TIME: 3 MIN.
SERVES 4

1 large bunch of fresh mint
1 tablespoon oil
2 green chillies (chili peppers)
2 red chillies (chili peppers)
1/2 teaspoon asafoetida powder
3 teaspoons black gram dal (washed urad dal),
picked over and rinsed

2 teaspoons brown mustard seeds
a marble-sized piece of tamarind pulp
salt to taste
a little water

Method

Remove the stems from the mint leaves and discard. Dry-roast the mint leaves in a heavy saucepan, for about 5 minutes or until the leaves become fragrant.

Heat 1 tablespoon oil in a heavy frying pan or skillet. Add the 2 green chillies, 2 red chillies, asafoetida powder, black gram dal, and mustard seeds. Sauté until the black gram dal turns golden.

Place in an electric blender or food processor. Add the roasted mint leaves, tamarind pulp, and salt to taste. Blend into a fine paste, adding very little water.

Serve with hot rice, dosais, and vadais.

Coriander Chutney can be made the same way.

RIDGE GOURD PEEL CHUTNEY

Peerkangai Tholi Thuvaiyal

PREPARATION TIME: 25 MIN. COOKING TIME: 8 MIN.
SERVES 4

250 g (8 oz) ridge gourd (club or
sponge gourd, silk squash)
1 1/2 tablespoons oil
1 1/2 tablespoons black gram dal (washed urad dal),
picked over and rinsed
1 tablespoon Bengal gram dal (yellow split peas,
chana dal), picked over and rinsed
2 teaspoons brown mustard seeds
1/2 teaspoon asafoetida powder
2 red chillies (chili peppers)
3 green chillies (chili peppers)
1 small bunch of coriander (Chinese parsley) leaves
a marble-sized piece of tamarind pulp
salt to taste
a little water

OPPOSITE – *(clockwise from left) Mint Chutney, Brown Coconut Chutney, and Ridge Gourd Peel Chutney*

Method

Peel the ridge gourd. Do not discard the peel, but chop finely. Set the chopped peel aside.

Heat 2 teaspoons oil in a heavy frying pan or skillet. Add the black gram dal, Bengal gram dal, mustard seeds, asafoetida powder, red chillies, and green chillies. Sauté for 2–3 minutes. Set aside.

Using the remaining oil, sauté the chopped ridge gourd peel for 3–4 minutes.

Place both the dal mixture and the sautéed ridge gourd peel in an electric blender or food processor. Add the coriander leaves, tamarind pulp, salt to taste, and a little water. Blend ingredients into a fine paste.

Serve with hot rice and ghee.

This chutney is nothing short of inspired. It is made with the peel of the ridge gourd, which would normally be thrown away after a kootu is made with the vegetable marrow.

Also, when using snake gourd in a recipe, don't throw away the seeds. A chutney can be made from these seeds in the same way as the ridge gourd peel.

ONION CHUTNEY
Vengaya Thuvaiyal

PREPARATION TIME: 20 MIN. COOKING TIME: 5 MIN.
SERVES 4

2 tablespoons oil
2 teaspoons brown mustard seeds
4 teaspoons black gram dal (washed urad dal),
picked over and rinsed
2 red chillies (chili peppers)
3 green chillies (chili peppers)
1/2 teaspoon asafoetida powder
3 onions, finely chopped
1 small bunch of coriander (Chinese parsley) leaves
a marble-sized piece of tamarind pulp
salt to taste

Method

Heat 1 tablespoon oil in a heavy frying pan or skillet. Add mustard seeds, black gram dal, red chillies, green chillies, and asafoetida powder. Sauté for 2–3 minutes. Set aside.

Heat the remaining oil. Sauté chopped onions evenly until light golden in colour. Place both onions and seasoning in an electric blender or food processor. Add coriander leaves, tamarind pulp, and salt to taste. Blend to a fine paste.

Serve with hot rice and ghee.

LENTIL CHUTNEY
Parupu Thuvaiyal

PREPARATION TIME: 20 MIN. COOKING TIME: 3 MIN.
SERVES 4

2 tablespoons ghee
1/2 cup (3 oz) red gram dal (pigeon peas,
toor dal), picked over and rinsed
2 red chillies (chili peppers)
1/2 teaspoon asafoetida powder
4 tablespoons grated fresh coconut or
5 1/2 tablespoons flaked coconut
salt to taste

PREVIOUS PAGE – *Onion Chutney (top left), Eggplant Chutney (middle right), and Lentil Chutney (bottom left)*

Method

Heat 2 tablespoons ghee in a heavy frying pan or skillet. Sauté red gram dal, red chillies, and asafoetida powder until the red gram dal turns golden in colour.

Place this mixture in an electric blender or food processor. Add the grated coconut and salt to taste. Blend ingredients into a fine paste.

Serve with hot rice and ghee.

EGGPLANT CHUTNEY
Kathirikkai Thuvaiyal

PREPARATION TIME: 10 MIN. COOKING TIME: 10 MIN.
SERVES 4

6 teaspoons oil
1 large purple eggplant (aubergine)
2 teaspoons brown mustard seeds
1 teaspoon asafoetida powder
2 tablespoons black gram dal (washed urad dal),
picked over and rinsed
a lemon-sized piece of tamarind pulp
6–7 green chillies (chili peppers)
1 bunch of coriander (Chinese parsley) leaves
salt to taste

Method

Smear 2 teaspoons oil over the surface of the eggplant. Roast over a naked flame or grill until the skin is completely charred and the flesh soft. Remove skin and discard. Mash flesh well and set aside.

Heat 2 teaspoons oil in a heavy frying pan or skillet. Add mustard seeds and asafoetida powder. When the mustard seeds splutter, remove mixture from the pan. Set aside.

Take remaining 2 teaspoons oil and sauté the black gram dal. Set aside.

Place tamarind pulp, green chillies, coriander leaves, and sautéed mustard seeds and asafoetida powder in an electric blender or food processor. Add the mashed eggplant and salt to taste. Thoroughly blend for 1–2 minutes. Add the sautéed black gram dal. Blend for a further minute.

Serve with rice.

It is the black gram dal that gives this chutney its crunchy, nutty flavour. Do not blend it too finely when you add it to the chutney or you will lose this delicious texture.

CHOKO CHUTNEY
Chow Chow Thuvaiyal
**PREPARATION TIME: 20 MIN. COOKING TIME: 4 MIN.
SERVES 4**

1 tablespoon oil
1 medium-sized choko (chayote), peeled and grated
1 medium-sized tomato, finely chopped
1 green chilli (chili pepper)
a small bunch of coriander (Chinese parsley) leaves
2 teaspoons oil (extra)
2 tablespoons red gram dal (pigeon peas,
toor dal), picked over and rinsed
1 tablespoon black gram dal (washed urad dal),
picked over and rinsed
3 red chillies (chili peppers)
½ teaspoon asafoetida powder
salt to taste

Method

Heat 1 tablespoon oil in a heavy frying pan or skillet. Add the grated choko, finely chopped tomato, and green chilli. Lastly, add the coriander leaves. Sauté for 2–3 minutes.

Place this mixture in an electric blender or food processor. Do not add any water. Blend ingredients to a fine paste. Set aside.

Heat the extra oil in a heavy frying pan or skillet. Add the red gram dal, black gram dal, red chillies, and asafoetida powder. Sauté until the dals turn golden. Blend or process into a fine powder.

In an electric blender or food processor, blend this powder with the vegetable paste and salt to taste.

Serve with hot rice.

Use this basic recipe to make a chutney with any of your favourite vegetables. You can use almost any vegetable or herb — carrot, cabbage, kohlrabi, mint, eggplant, ridge gourd (club or sponge gourd, silk squash) or snake gourd.

OPPOSITE – *Instant Mango Pickle (top), Choko Chutney (bottom right), and Gooseberry Pickle (bottom left)*

GOOSEBERRY PICKLE
Ari Nellikkai Urugai
**PREPARATION TIME: 20 MIN. COOKING TIME: 20 MIN.
MAKES 1 SMALL BOTTLE**

1 cup (6 oz) cape or green gooseberries
½ teaspoon asafoetida powder
1 teaspoon fenugreek seeds
½ cup (4 fl oz) sesame oil
1½ teaspoons brown mustard seeds
½ teaspoon ground turmeric
4 teaspoons chilli powder
¼ cup (2 oz) salt

Method

Remove the seeds from the gooseberries. Chop and set aside.

Dry-roast the asafoetida powder and fenugreek seeds in a heavy saucepan for 2–3 minutes. Blend into a fine powder in an electric blender or food processor. Set aside.

Heat the sesame oil in a heavy frying pan or skillet. Add the mustard seeds, ground turmeric, and chilli powder. Sauté for 2–3 minutes. Add the chopped gooseberries, salt and asafoetida/fenugreek mixture. Mix thoroughly. Remove from the heat. Do not overcook.

Cool completely before storing in an airtight container.

INSTANT MANGO PICKLE
Uppu Pisiri Mangai
**PREPARATION TIME: 15 MIN. COOKING TIME: 3 MIN.
SERVES 4**

1 green mango
salt to taste
2 teaspoons chilli powder
½ teaspoon ground turmeric
1 teaspoon asafoetida powder

FOR TEMPERING

2 tablespoons oil
2 teaspoons brown mustard seeds

Method

Peel and dice the mango into 1 cm (½ in) pieces.

Place the mango, salt, chilli powder, ground turmeric, and asafoetida powder in a bowl.

TEMPERING: Heat 2 tablespoons oil in a heavy frying pan or skillet. Add the mustard seeds.

When the mustard seeds splutter, add to the mango mixture. Mix thoroughly.

Serve with rice and plain yogurt.

This pickle will keep for a couple of days if refrigerated.

GRATED MANGO PICKLE
Mangai Thokku

PREPARATION TIME: 30 MIN. COOKING TIME: 15 MIN.
MAKES 1 MEDIUM BOTTLE

4 large green mangoes
1 teaspoon fenugreek seeds
1 teaspoon asafoetida powder
1/2 cup (4 fl oz) sesame oil
2 teaspoons brown mustard seeds
1/4 cup (1 oz) chilli powder
1/2 teaspoon ground turmeric
1/4 cup (2 oz) salt

Method

Peel and grate the mangoes. Set aside.

Dry-roast the fenugreek seeds and asafoetida powder in a heavy saucepan for 3–4 minutes. Blend to a fine powder in an electric blender or food processor. Set aside.

Heat 1/2 cup (4 fl oz) sesame oil in a heavy frying pan or skillet. Add the mustard seeds. When they splutter, add the chilli powder and ground turmeric. Sauté for 1 minute.

Add the grated mango, salt and fenugreek/asafoetida mixture. Continue cooking until the oil floats on top.

Allow to cool completely and store in a bottle.

This pickle will last for a month when stored in the refrigerator.

HOT LEMON PICKLE
Elumichai Urugai

PREPARATION TIME: 10 MIN. COOKING TIME: 40 MIN.
MAKES 1 SMALL BOTTLE

1 teaspoon fenugreek seeds
1/2 teaspoon asafoetida powder
6 lemons
water to cover
3/4 cup (6 fl oz) sesame oil
1 teaspoon brown mustard seeds
4 teaspoons red chilli powder
6 green chillies (chili peppers), chopped
a piece of fresh ginger (4 cm/1 1/2 in long), scraped and finely chopped
1/2 teaspoon ground turmeric
8 tablespoons salt

Method

Dry-roast the fenugreek seeds and asafoetida powder in a heavy saucepan for about 2–3 minutes. Blend into a fine powder in an electric blender or food processor. Set aside.

Place the whole lemons in a saucepan. Add sufficient water to cover them, and bring to the boil. Boil for 10–15 minutes, or until tender. Allow the lemons to cool, quarter and set aside. Also reserve the cooking water.

Heat 3/4 cup (6 fl oz) oil in a heavy frying pan or skillet. Add the mustard seeds.

When the mustard seeds splutter, add the chilli powder, green chillies, ginger and ground turmeric. Sauté for 2–3 minutes. Add the quartered lemons and reserved cooking water.

Now add the 8 tablespoons salt and the fenugreek/asafoetida mixture. Cook for a few minutes until well blended.

Store in an airtight bottle and refrigerate.

MANGO PICKLE
Avakkai

PREPARATION TIME: 1 WEEK
MAKES 1 LARGE JAR

25 medium-sized green mangoes
1 tablespoon cumin seeds
1 1/2 cups (12 oz) salt
1 1/2 cups (6 oz) red chilli powder
1 cup (5 oz) brown mustard seeds
5 cups (40 fl oz) sesame oil
2 teaspoons fenugreek seeds
1 tablespoon asafoetida powder
1 tablespoon ground turmeric

Method

Cut the mangoes, including the hard seed, into at least 16 pieces per mango. Wash and spread the mango pieces on a cloth to dry for about 1 hour, preferably in the sun.

Dry-roast the cumin seeds in a heavy saucepan, for 2–3 minutes. Blend into a fine powder in an electric blender or food processor.

In a large bowl, mix together the salt, chilli powder, and mustard seeds.

Heat 5 cups (40 fl oz) sesame oil in a large, heavy saucepan. Allow to cool completely. Add the salt/chilli powder/mustard seed mixture, taking care that no lumps are formed.

Gradually add the cut mangoes, stirring constantly. Now add the fenugreek seeds, cumin seeds, asafoetida powder, and ground turmeric. Mix thoroughly.

Store in an airtight jar. On alternate days, turn the pickle well. It will be ready for use in 1 week.

DRIED CHILLI
Moru Milagai

PREPARATION TIME: APPROX. 1 WEEK
MAKES 250 G (8 OZ)

2 tablespoons fenugreek seeds
½ cup (4 fl oz) water
6 cups (48 fl oz) plain yogurt (see p. 136)
4 cups (32 oz) salt
4 cups (8 oz) green chillies (chili peppers),
slit sideways without removing the stalks

Method

Soak the fenugreek seeds in ½ cup (4 fl oz) water for 30 minutes. Blend into a fine paste in an electric blender or food processor.

In a large bowl, mix the yogurt with the salt and the fenugreek paste.

Soak the slit green chillies in this yogurt mixture for 3–4 days. Shake the vessel every day.

On the fourth day, remove the green chillies and dry in the sun for the whole day. In the evening, resoak the partly dried green chillies in the yogurt mixture.

The following day, remove the chillies and dry in the sun once again. Resoak them in the evening. Continue this process every day until the yogurt has been completely absorbed.

Dry the green chillies in the sun until they turn cream in colour.

Store in an airtight container and use as required. Deep-fry in oil until black in colour before using.

Serve with Curd Rice (see p. 76).

These perky dried chillies will keep for a whole year.

GREEN CHILLI PICKLE
Milagai Thokku

PREPARATION TIME: 10 MIN. COOKING TIME: 20 MIN.
MAKES APPROX. 200 G (7 OZ)

2 tablespoons oil
2 teaspoons brown mustard seeds
3 cups green chillies (chili peppers)
a large lemon-sized piece of tamarind pulp
2 tablespoons powdered jaggery
1 large bunch of coriander (Chinese parsley) leaves
salt to taste

Method

Heat 2 tablespoons oil in a heavy frying pan or skillet. Add the mustard seeds. When they splutter, add the green chillies. Sauté for 2–3 minutes.

Place this mixture in an electric blender or food processor. Add the tamarind pulp, powdered jaggery, coriander leaves, and salt to taste. Blend ingredients into a coarse paste. Do not use water.

Store in an airtight container.

Serve with dosais and Curd Rice (see p. 76).

This pickle will last for a week if kept in the refrigerator.

OPPOSITE – *Green Chilli Pickle (in bowl)*
and Dried Chilli (scattered)
PREVIOUS PAGE – *(clockwise from left) Mango Pickle, Grated Mango*
Pickle, and Hot Lemon Pickle

BASIC
RECIPES

The following basic recipes are fundamental to South Indian cooking. Whether it be yogurt, curry powder or sambar powder, each of these ingredients is an essential component of authentic South Indian cuisine.

~

While there is no doubt you can buy sambar powder or rasam powder off the shelf today, there's nothing like making your own. For those who enjoy the flavour of copra, I have included an unusual sambar powder made with this ingredient.

~

Curry powder is yet another special recipe of mine. Just a sprinkling of it enlivens the flavour of even the most ordinary vegetable dish.

Sambar Powder 1
Sambar Podi 1

PREPARATION TIME: 30 MIN.
MAKES 200 G (7 OZ)

1 tablespoon oil
2 cups (approx. 2 oz) red chillies (chili peppers)
1¾ cups (5 oz) coriander seeds
4 tablespoons cumin seeds
1½ tablespoons fenugreek seeds
1½ tablespoons black peppercorns
1½ tablespoons brown mustard seeds
2 teaspoons Bengal gram dal (yellow split peas,
chana dal), picked over and rinsed
2 teaspoons red gram dal (pigeon peas, toor dal),
picked over and rinsed
2 teaspoons poppy seeds
2 large sticks cinnamon bark
a few curry leaves
2 teaspoons ground turmeric

Method

Heat 1 tablespoon oil in a heavy frying pan or skillet. Add the red chillies and sauté for 2–3 minutes.

In a heavy saucepan, one at a time, dry-roast the coriander seeds, cumin seeds, fenugreek seeds, black peppercorns, mustard seeds, Bengal gram dal, red gram dal, poppy seeds, cinnamon bark and a few curry leaves, until they each give off a strong aroma. (However, do *not* roast the ground turmeric.)

Place all the ingredients in an electric blender or food processor. Blend into a fine powder.

Store in an airtight container and use as required.

Sambar Powder 2
Sambar Podi 2

PREPARATION TIME: 30 MIN.
MAKES 400 G (14 OZ)

2 cups (6 oz) coriander seeds
2 cups (approx. 2 oz) red chillies (chili peppers)
4 tablespoons black peppercorns
4 tablespoons cumin seeds
2 teaspoons fenugreek seeds
2 teaspoons brown mustard seeds
½ cup (3 oz) Bengal gram dal (yellow split peas,
chana dal), picked over and rinsed
2 teaspoons poppy seeds
1 copra, grated (approx. ½–¾ cup grated copra)
1 large stick cinnamon bark
1 large bunch of curry leaves
2 teaspoons ground turmeric

Method

In a heavy saucepan, dry-roast all the ingredients separately, until they each give off a strong aroma. (However, do *not* roast the ground turmeric.)

Place all the ingredients in an electric blender or food processor. Blend into a fine powder.

Store in an airtight container and use as required.

Plain Yogurt
Dahi

PREPARATION TIME: 15 MIN. SETTING TIME: 6–8 HOURS
MAKES 4 CUPS (32 FL OZ)

4 cups (1 litre, 32 fl oz) milk
2 tablespoons plain yogurt

Method

Quickly bring the milk to the boil in a heavy saucepan, stirring constantly.

Transfer milk to a large container that has been sterilised with hot water. Set aside to cool. While still warm, add the yogurt. Mix thoroughly. Cover with a clean cloth or a lid. Keep in a warm place for 6–8 hours until set. The yogurt should be thick and firm.

Chill in a refrigerator and use as required.

OPPOSITE – *(from bottom to top) Sambar Powder 1, Sambar Powder 2, and Plain Yogurt*

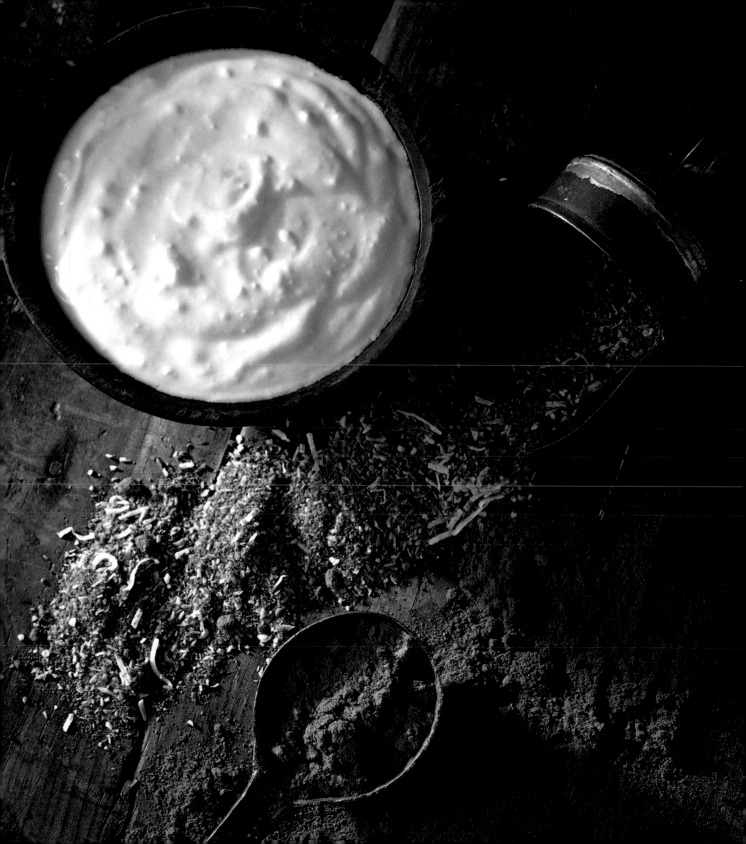

RASAM POWDER
Rasam Podi

PREPARATION TIME: 30 MIN.
MAKES 450 G (15 OZ)

2¹/₂ cups (7 oz) coriander seeds
1¹/₄ cups (1¹/₂ oz) red chillies (chili peppers)
³/₄ cup (5 oz) red gram dal (pigeon peas, toor dal),
picked over and rinsed
4 tablespoons Bengal gram dal (yellow split peas,
chana dal), picked over and rinsed

¹/₂ cup (3 oz) black peppercorns
¹/₂ tablespoon cumin seeds
1 small bunch of curry leaves
1 teaspoon ground turmeric

Method

In a heavy saucepan, dry-roast all the ingredients separately, until they each give off a strong aroma. (However, do *not* roast the ground turmeric.)

Place all the ingredients in an electric blender or food processor. Blend into a fine powder.

Store in an airtight container and use as required.

MYSORE RASAM POWDER
Mysore Rasam Podi

PREPARATION TIME: 20 MIN.
MAKES 200 G (7 OZ)

2 cups (6 oz) coriander seeds
4 tablespoons black peppercorns
4 tablespoons cumin seeds
4 teaspoons fenugreek seeds
1 bunch of curry leaves
3 teaspoons oil
2 cups (2 oz) red chillies (chili peppers)
2 teaspoons ground turmeric

Method

In a heavy saucepan, dry-roast the coriander seeds, black peppercorns, cumin seeds, fenugreek seeds, and curry leaves until fragrant (about 5 minutes). Set aside.

Heat 3 teaspoons oil in a heavy frying pan or skillet. Add the red chillies and sauté for 2–3 minutes.

Place all the ingredients, including the ground turmeric, in an electric blender or food processor. Blend into a fine powder.

Store in an airtight container and use as required.

CURRY POWDER
Curry Podi

PREPARATION TIME: 10 MIN. COOKING TIME: 5 MIN.
MAKES 200 G (7 OZ)

1¼ cups (4 oz) coriander seeds
¾ cup (5 oz) Bengal gram dal (yellow split peas, chana dal), picked over and rinsed
½ cup (3 oz) black gram dal (washed urad dal), picked over and rinsed
3 teaspoons oil
¾ cup (1 oz) red chillies (chili peppers)
2 teaspoons asafoetida powder
a marble-sized piece of tamarind pulp
salt to taste

Method

In a heavy saucepan, dry-roast the coriander seeds, Bengal gram dal and black gram dal for about 5 minutes.

Heat 3 teaspoons oil in a heavy frying pan or skillet. Add the red chillies and sauté for 2–3 minutes.

Place all the ingredients in an electric blender or food processor, including asafoetida powder, tamarind pulp and salt to taste. Blend into a fine powder.

Store in an airtight container and use as required.

This powder is used for poriyals such as Colocasia Roast, Plantain Poriyal, Yam Poriyal, etc.

DOSAI CHILLI POWDER
Dosai Milagai Podi

PREPARATION TIME: 10 MIN. COOKING TIME: 8 MIN.
MAKES 150 G (5 OZ)

2 teaspoons oil
1¼ cups (1½ oz) red chillies (chili peppers)
½ cup (3 oz) black gram dal (washed urad dal), picked over and rinsed
½ cup (3 oz) Bengal gram dal (yellow split peas, chana dal), picked over and rinsed
1 teaspoon asafoetida powder
4 tablespoons white sesame seeds
2 tablespoons powdered jaggery
a marble-sized piece of tamarind pulp (optional)
salt to taste

Method

Heat 2 teaspoons oil in a heavy frying pan or skillet. Add the red chillies and sauté for 2–3 minutes.

In a heavy saucepan, dry-roast the black gram dal, Bengal gram dal, asafoetida powder, and sesame seeds for about 5 minutes.

Place all the ingredients, including the jaggery, tamarind pulp (if used), and salt to taste, in an electric blender or food processor. Blend into a coarse powder.

Store in an airtight container and use as required.

Dosai Chilli Powder makes an excellent accompaniment to dosais and idlis.

OPPOSITE – *Rasam Powder, Mysore Rasam Powder, Curry Powder, and Dosai Chilli Powder*

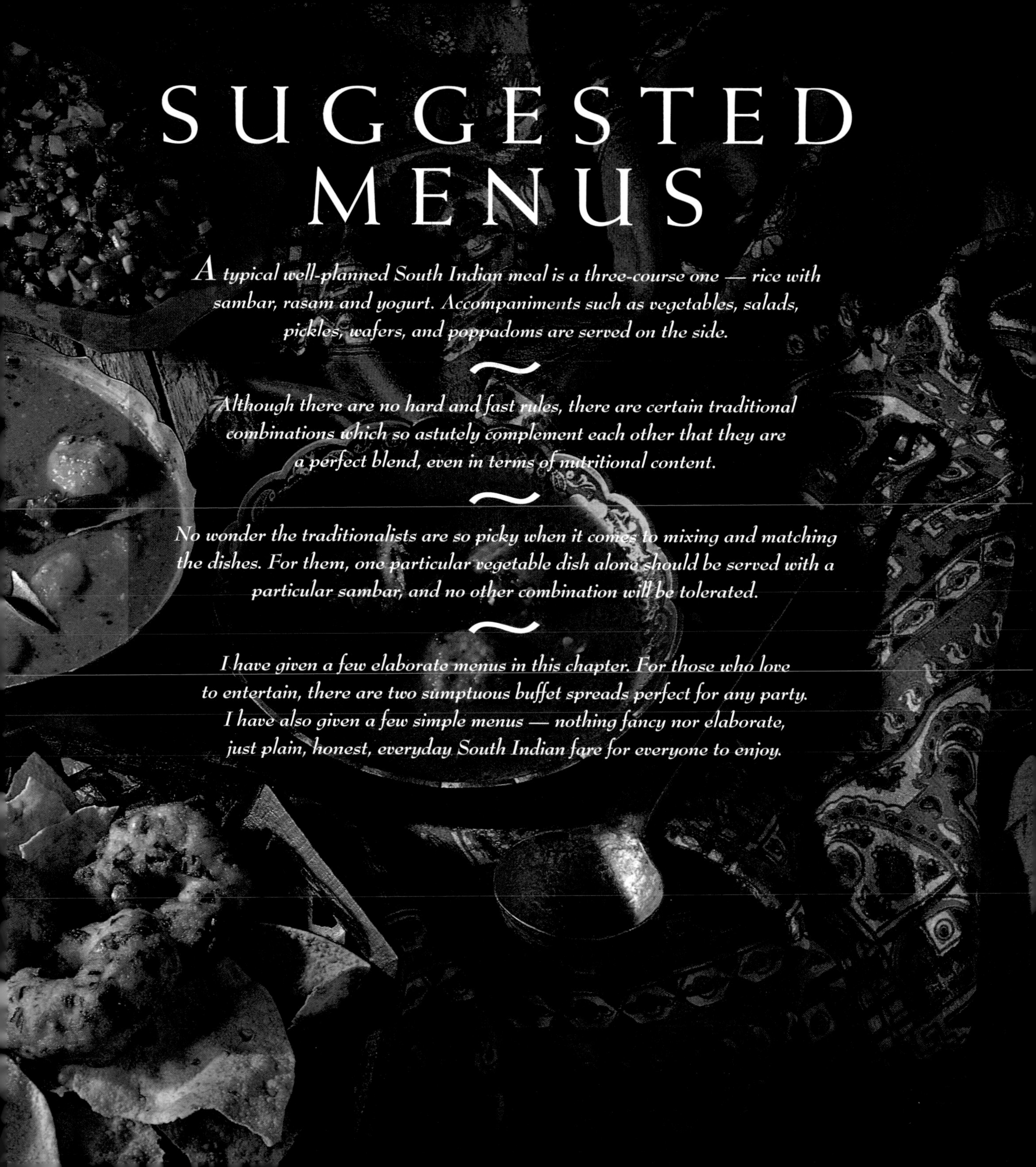

SUGGESTED MENUS

A typical well-planned South Indian meal is a three-course one — rice with sambar, rasam and yogurt. Accompaniments such as vegetables, salads, pickles, wafers, and poppadoms are served on the side.

~

Although there are no hard and fast rules, there are certain traditional combinations which so astutely complement each other that they are a perfect blend, even in terms of nutritional content.

~

No wonder the traditionalists are so picky when it comes to mixing and matching the dishes. For them, one particular vegetable dish alone should be served with a particular sambar, and no other combination will be tolerated.

~

I have given a few elaborate menus in this chapter. For those who love to entertain, there are two sumptuous buffet spreads perfect for any party. I have also given a few simple menus — nothing fancy nor elaborate, just plain, honest, everyday South Indian fare for everyone to enjoy.

MENU I

Rice

Small Onion Sambar (p. 2)

Tomato Rasam (p. 20)

Colocasia Roast (p. 40)

Bean Poriyal (p. 32)

Coconut Curd Salad (p. 61)

Plain Yogurt (p. 136)

Instant Mango Pickle (p. 128)

Fried Poppadoms

Vermicelli Payasam (p. 110)

MENU II

Rice

Buttermilk Sambar (p. 6)

Mysore Rasam (p. 28)

Yam Poriyal (p. 34)

Cabbage Poriyal (p. 35)

Carrot Salad (see Vegetable Medley, p. 58)

Mashed Amaranth (p. 51)

Plain Yogurt (p. 136)

Grated Mango Pickle (p. 130)

Fried Poppadoms

Milk Payasam (p. 110)

MENU III

Spicy Sambar Rice (p. 74)

Lemon Rasam (p. 23)

Potato Roast (see Colocasia Roast, p. 40)

Cabbage Poriyal (p. 35)

Okra Curd Salad (p. 62)

Curd Rice (p. 76)

Yam Chips (p. 106)

Gooseberry Pickle (p. 128)

Almond Payasam (p. 112)

MENU IV

Rice
Dumpling Sambar (p. 13)
Drumstick Rasam (p. 26)
Plantain Stem Poriyal (p. 35)
Mashed Potato Poriyal (p. 36)
Mixed Vegetable Curd Salad (p. 61)
Plain Yogurt (p. 136)
Hot Lemon Pickle (p. 130)
Fried Poppadoms
Creamy Milk Pudding (p. 112)

BUFFET
SPREAD I

BUFFET
SPREAD II

Green Pea Rice (p. 71)

Lemon Rice (p. 66)

Potato Song (p. 52)

Vegetable Korma (p. 52)

Masala Dosai (p. 87)

Small Onion Sambar (p. 2)

Coconut Chutney 2 (p. 122)

Bean Poriyal (p. 32)

Vegetable Medley (p. 58)

Curd Vadai (p. 98)

Curd Rice (p. 76)

Instant Mango Pickle (p. 128)

Fried Poppadoms

Puris

Carrot & Cashew Payasam (p. 110)

SIMPLE
MENU I

Rice
Mysore Rasam (p. 28)
Onion Chutney (p. 127)
Sweet Pepper Poriyal (p. 32)
Fresh Cucumber Salad (p. 58)
Plain Yogurt (p. 136)
Roasted Poppadoms

SIMPLE
MENU II

Rice
Brown Coconut Chutney (p. 124)
Spicy Lentil Rasam (p. 28)
Plantain Stem Poriyal (p. 35)
Vegetable Medley (p. 58)
Plain Yogurt (p. 136)
Fried Poppadoms

SIMPLE MENU III

Rice
Curry Leaf Sambar (p. 9)
Bean Dal Poriyal (p. 36)
Ordinary Rasam (p. 20)
Mango Curd Salad (p. 62)
Plain Yogurt (p. 136)
Roasted Poppadoms

SIMPLE MENU IV

Rice
Tamarind Kootu (p. 44)
Tomato Rasam (p. 20)
Okra Curd Salad (p. 62)
Mashed Potato Poriyal (p. 36)
Fried Poppadoms

GLOSSARY
Ingredients

Amaranth: a nutritious annual plant with a sweetish flavour. High in protein. Both its leaves and seeds can be used. Available from better greengrocers, or Asian and West Indian food stores.

Aniseed: also known as anise seed. A member of the parsley family, this seed has a distinctive liquorice flavour.

Ash gourd: one of the gourd family, ash gourd is treated in the same way as bitter gourd or melon. Available from Asian food stores.

Asafoetida powder: made from the dried resin of several fennel-like plants, asafoetida is then ground for use in cooking. This is a very pungent spice with a strong aroma, so use sparingly.

Bay leaves: also known as laurel leaf or bay laurel, these leaves are the foliage of the evergreen bay laurel tree. This aromatic herb is available both fresh and dried, with the fresh leaves being superior in flavour, but less commonly available.

Bangal gram dal: also known as yellow split peas or chana dal, Bengal gram dal is split and the skins removed. A small variety of the chickpea, this pale yellow dal is often used in the classic Indian dish, dal. Available from Indian or Middle Eastern grocery stores. Bengal gram dal can also often be found in supermarkets or health food stores.

Besan: also known as chickpea flour and Bengal gram flour, besan is ground from Bengal gram dal (yellow split peas, chana dal). This flour is used both as a thickener and a binding agent in Indian cooking. Besan has its own distinctive flavour and cannot be substituted by ordinary wheat flour.

Bitter gourd: also known as bitter melon or balsam pear. With its crinkly green skin, it looks something like a cucumber and is available from Asian food stores, fresh or canned.

Black gram dal: also known as washed urad dal, black gram dal is split urad beans with their skins removed. A pale cream in colour, black gram dal is much used in South Indian cooking. Available from Indian or Middle Eastern grocery stores.

Black peppercorns: the dried fruit of *Piper nigrum*, a vine native to India. Use whole in vegetable and rice dishes.

Buttermilk: the liquid left behind after cream has been separated into butter. In South India, ½ cup (4 fl oz) mixed with 1 cup (8 fl oz) water and beaten well is referred to as 'buttermilk'. Thick buttermilk is made by adding less water.

Cape gooseberry: this berry grows wild throughout mainland USA, but it is widely cultivated in Hawaii, Australia, New Zealand, India and China. Green when unripe, it turns an opaque golden yellow colour when ripe.

Cardamom pods: related to ginger, cardamom is a spice native to India. Often used in desserts, it is highly fragrant with a spicy flavour. Cardamom pods contain the seeds from which ground cardamom is made.

Chillies (fresh & dried): also known as chilli peppers, this fruit is available in many shapes and sizes, dried or fresh (according to season). Red and green chillies are used in this book. Be careful when chopping fresh chilli as it can easily burn your skin.

Chilli powder: ripe red chillies that have been dried, and then ground into a powder. It should not be mistaken for Mexican chilli powder.

Choko: also known as chayote or mirliton, this squash-like fruit is around the size and shape of a pear. Its flesh is white, and is covered in a furrowed uneven, light green skin.

Chutney: a spicy side dish, made with many types of fruit and vegetables, used as a condiment for other dishes. In South India, both chutneys and pickles are often made with unripe green mangoes.

Cinnamon bark: this fragrant spice is used in both stick and ground form. Used extensively in South Indian cooking.

Coconut: from the palm of the same name, the coconut comes in several readily available forms. It can be bought fresh or in dried (copra), desiccated, shredded or flaked form.

Coconut milk: can be store-bought or made at home using equal parts of shredded fresh or desiccated coconut meat. Place in a bowl with 1½ cups (12 fl oz) hot water. Cover and let stand until water has cooled.

Strain through a fine sieve or cloth (e.g. muslin), squeezing out as much liquid as possible. Store in refrigerator. *Coconut cream* is made in the same way, but with 1 part water to 4 parts coconut meat.

Coconut oil: pressed from copra or dried coconut meat.

Colocasia: a white, starchy vegetable rather like yam. Available canned from Asian food stores if you are unable to buy fresh colocasia. Yam or sweet potato can be used as substitutes.

Copra: dried coconut meat, from which coconut oil is extracted. The coconut kernel is dried in the sun, and it is from this dried flesh that the oil is pressed.

Coriander (fresh): also known as Chinese parsley or cilantro, this herb is used extensively both as an ingredient and as a garnish in South Indian cooking.

Coriander seed: a spice commonly used in both vegetable and meat dishes. These seeds are also one of the ingredients used in sambar, rasam and curry powders, and also in garam masala.

Cumin seed: shaped like a caraway seed, this spice has its own unique taste. Often tempered in hot oil to flavour vegetable and rice dishes.

Curry leaves: the leaves of the plant *Murraya koenigii.* With a flavour remiscent of curry powder, these leaves are almost a staple ingredient in South Indian cooking. However, despite their name, curry powder is *not* ground from curry leaves. Available fresh or dried.

Dal: Indian name for lentils or pulses, the term 'dal' covers all dried peas and beans. Dals are consumed in both the north and south of India. In South India, dals are used in many recipes, and are an excellent source of protein.

Drumstick: an Indian vegetable rather like squash, but with a long, skinny shape (as its name suggests). Drumstick may be available fresh in some places, or canned from Indian markets or Asian food stores.

Eggplant: also known as aubergine, this vegetable has a glossy dark-purple skin and off-white flesh.

Fenugreek seed: a strong aromatic spice, fenugreek seeds are often used in South Indian dishes. Be sure to only use the required amount as their bitter flavour can be overpowering.

Fried gram dal: this dal is roasted and puffed Bengal gram dal (yellow split peas, chana dal). It should be available from Indian markets or Asian food stores. If not, use dry-roasted Bengal gram dal instead.

Ghee: a form of clarified butter, ghee is pure butter fat, and therefore suitable for frying and sautéing at extremely high temperatures as all milk solids have been removed. You can make your own ghee using the following method: Take 500 g (1 lb) of unsalted butter and melt in a heavy saucepan, over a low heat. Gently simmer until all the moisture has evaporated and the milk solids have separated from the clear butter fat. Stir continuously during

simmering to prevent the butter from browning. Remove from heat. Strain the ghee through a fine muslin cloth. Allow to cool and store in a refrigerator.

Ginger (fresh): well known for its distinctive sharp taste, ginger is widely used in Indian cooking. Scrape off the skin before using, and chip, grate or slice as desired.

Ginger (ground): use where stipulated only. Ground ginger should *not* be substituted for fresh ginger.

Golden shallots: also known simply as shallots, these are the bulb of the plant *Allium ascalonicum.* Small, slightly purple onions with red–brown skin, shallots grow in clusters similar to garlic.

Green gram dal: also known as split mung beans or moong dal, green gram dal is actually pale yellow in colour. Split and without husks, this dal never needs to be soaked before cooking. Available from health food stores or Indian and Middle Eastern grocery stores.

Green mango: this term simply refers to the unripened fruit of any variety of mango tree. Much prized in India and often used in pickles and chutneys.

Jaggery: not to be mistaken for palm sugar or 'gur', this is a coarse, dark, unrefined sugar made from the juice of crushed sugar cane. Available in several forms, it commonly comes as a solid cake, which can then be powdered for use in cooking. Available from Indian markets or Asian food stores.

Masala: a 'mixture' or blend of herbs, spices and seasonings. A masala can be a paste or a powder, and can be made in any number of combinations from any number of ingredients.

Mustard seed (brown): brownish-black in colour, these seeds come from the annual plant *Brassica juncea*. They are a vital element of South Indian cooking, and are usually tempered in hot oil to bring out their nutty flavour.

Okra: also known as lady's fingers. Its green pods are tapered in shape, rather like chillies, with a ridged skin.

Plain yogurt (dahi): also known as natural yogurt or Indian curd, Indian yogurt is thick and creamy, and simple to make. Store-bought yogurt can be used as a substitute, but the flavour is not as fine as that of freshly made yogurt.

Plantain: also known as cooking banana, and widely used in South Indian cooking. Plantains are larger than sweet, eating bananas, with a thick, green skin and starchy interior.

Poppy seed: the dried seeds of the poppy plant. Poppy seeds add a nutty flavour to dishes. In Indian cooking, they are often ground into a fine powder and then used as a thickening agent in place of flour.

Ragi flour: ragi is a red grain largely cultivated in southern India. Its Latin name is *Eleusine coracana gaertu*. Ragi flour cannot be substituted by any other flour, but should be available in Indian markets or Asian food stores.

Red gram dal: also known as pigeon peas or toor dal, this dal is pale yellow to gold in colour, and used skinned and split. Do not confuse with red lentils. Used widely in South Indian cooking, especially sambars. Available from Indian and Middle Eastern grocery stores.

Rice flour: flour made from ground rice.

Ridge gourd: also known as club gourd, sponge gourd, and silk squash, this vegetable belongs to the cucumber family. Its ridged skin is removed before eating. Available at Asian grocery stores and some greengrocers.

Rock candy: also known as sugar candy. It is made by slowly evaporating concentrated sugar syrup into chunks.

Saffron: the stigmas of the small purple crocus, *Crocus sativa*, saffron threads are picked by hand. This labor-intensive process helps to make saffron the world's most expensive spice. Strongly perfumed with an unusual sweet–sharp tase, saffron adds both flavour and its characteristic colour to dishes.

Semolina: made from durum wheat, semolina is the coarsely ground part of the grain that is left behind when the finer flour is sifted out. It is usually available in three grades — fine, medium and coarse.

Sesame oil: also known as gingelly oil. Sesame oil is pressed from the seeds of the same name. Widely used in South Indian cooking.

Sesame seed: this seed has been eaten throughout India for thousands of years. Nutty in flavour, it is often used in vegetable and rice dishes, chutneys, pickles, and desserts. White sesame seeds are widely used in South Indian cooking.

Snake gourd: similar to the bitter gourd or melon, but with a coiling shape reminiscent of a snake. Available from Asian food stores.

Spring onions: also known as scallions or green onions (and sometimes wrongly as shallots). Spring onions have an immature base, not fully developed into a bulb, and long, straight, green leaves.

Sweet pepper: also known as capsicum, this term covers a number of mild peppers in the *Capsicum* genus, ranging in colour from light to dark green, and yellow to orange and red.

Sweet potato: also known as kumara and sometimes, mistakenly, yam. Can range in colour from white to the reddish orange of kumara.

Tamarind: also known as Indian date. The fruit of a large tree native to India, tamarind is commonly available in three forms: pulp, concentrate and sauce. Tamarind pulp or cake is available from Asian food stores. If using tamarind concentrate, adjust recipe quantities according to the packet instructions.

Turmeric (ground): a relative of the ginger plant, this spice adds the yellow colour to curry powder. Turmeric is one of the essential ingredients of Indian regional cooking. Use sparingly as it can be bitter in flavour.

Vermicelli: very thin strands of pasta.

Yam: often mistaken for sweet potato, yam is a starchy vegetable which is cooked in a similar manner. Its skin is tough and barky, and yam flesh can vary in colour from off-white to purple.

Cooking Utensils

Idli mould: an individual concave mould (similar to a madeleine mould, but without the scallops), in which idli dumplings are placed for cooking. If you do not have an idli mould or stand, you can shape these delicious dumplings with your hands and cook in a steamer or on a steamer stand. Available from Asian grocery stores.

Idli stand: also known as an idli tree, this piece of equipment is often tiered, and allows you to cook several idlis at once. A single layer rather resembles an egg poacher, but with a central stem, which allows you to steam the idlis in a large saucepan filled with 2½ cm (1 in) if water. Made from stainless steel or aluminium, and available from Asian grocery stores. If you do not have an idli stand, improvise with a steamer stand placed in a large saucepan.

Tawa: always made of cast-iron, this slightly concave griddle looks a little like a cast-iron skillet, and often has a wooden handle. It is used for dry-roasting and tempering spices, and cooking dosais and flat breads such as parathas. Never put your tawa away without seasoning with oil.

This helps to prevent rust. If you do not have a tawa, a griddle or cast-iron skillet can be used instead. Available from Asian grocery stores.

Indian Terms

Adai: a pancake, thicker than a dosai. An adai is made with two or three dals which have been ground to a paste, and shallow-fried until golden in colour.

Bajji: this is a vegetable fritter, dipped in a batter and deep-fried. It is usually eaten as a snack.

Bonda: vegetable mixtures shaped into balls, and then dipped in a batter and deep-fried. Commonly made with a potato filling.

Burfi: a toffee commonly made from peanuts, besan, coconut, or milk.

Chapatti: an Indian bread made from whole-wheat (wholemeal) flour.

Dosai: a crisp pancake commonly made from rice and dal, semolina, or wholewheat (wholemeal) flour.

Idli: steamed dumplings made from rice and dal, semolina etc.

Kootu: a dish where a vegetable is combined with a dal. Neither wet nor dry, but something in between, kootus can be served as side dishes or eaten with rice.

Laddu: a ball-shaped fudge commonly made from semolina, sesame seeds, or besan.

Oothappam: made from dosai batter, an oothappam is a thicker pancake than a dosai, and is topped with different garnishes.

Pakora: a light snack made from onions, besan, etc., and deep-fried in oil.

Paratha: an Indian bread that is shallow-fried on a tawa or griddle.

Payasam: a southern dessert made from milk simmered with crushed cashews, cereals and sugar, and topped with sautéed raisins.

Pongal: a rice and dal 'kedgeree' spiced with pepper, cumin seeds, and freshly grated ginger.

Poppadom: also known as an 'appalam' in South India. Poppadoms are thin, round wafers (about 15 cm [6 in] in diameter) made from dal. They can be served deep-fried or roasted over an open flame. Poppadoms can be bought plain, or flavoured with red (cayenne) pepper or garlic.

Poriyal: a dry vegetable dish, usually served without a gravy.

Puri: a deep-fried Indian bread. A puri puffs up like a balloon while frying. Its outside is crisp and the inside soft.

Rasam: a South Indian version of soup. Mostly eaten with rice, the rasam forms the second course in a typical South Indian meal.

Sambar: a soup-like dal and vegetable dish, with a tamarind flavour.

Vadai: a deep-fried doughnut made of lentils, potatoes, sago, etc.

INDEX

Numbers in italics refer to illustrations